MINDFULNESS JOURNAL
for Busy Moms

ANNE MARIE O'CONNOR

CENTENNIAL BOOKS

MINDFULNESS JOURNAL
for Busy Moms

CONTENTS

FINDING CENTER

As a mom, we know you're beyond busy. But embracing some simple, mindful practices can make your day more manageable.

There are millions of moments to stop and savor when you are a mom. The thrill of holding your baby for the very first time, the way her tiny hand will clutch your index finger, the gentle rise and fall of his chest as he sleeps. And as your children get older, there's no shortage of memories that you'll want to capture and hold onto— the first giggle, first step, first words, first friends, first day of school—the list goes on and on. Noticing moments big and small is all a part of motherhood.

But more often than not, we get caught up in the swirling whirlpool that is being a parent, from jam-packed days to sleepless nights. And the stress can take its toll, especially on those of us who are also juggling work and family matters. One British study of more than 6,000 people found women who have two kids and are also working full time have chronic stress levels that are 40 percent higher than working women who don't have children. (And that research was done before a worldwide pandemic put most moms into constant overdrive!) But you don't have to be working outside the home to feel the strain—just getting through the day as a full-time caregiver can be plenty of pressure.

We know that chronic stress is bad for you. It can put a strain on your body, leading to illnesses like heart disease, high blood pressure and diabetes, and it can affect your mental health, including disorders like depression and anxiety. At the very least, many moms are simply exhausted by everything we've got piled in front of us.

That's where mindfulness can help. Even taking just five minutes a day to practice some form of mindful activity—whether it's taking a walk, doing some deep breathing or just really appreciating a hot cup of coffee in the morning—can make a big difference in your overall well-being. Finding some simple ways to connect with yourself and with your family can be enough to help you stay centered, even when everything around you (children shouting, dog barking, dishes piling up, phone buzzing) seems like it's all spinning out of control.

This book offers plenty of strategies and support to help you tune in, calm down and find your focus. Whether it's some simple deep-breathing exercises (page 40); the beneficial effects of thinking positive (page 52) or easy yoga, Pilates and meditation how-to's (page 56), there are plenty of ways to help you connect with yourself. And then there's journaling—the process of recording your thoughts, feelings, anxieties and desires—which can have a tremendous number of benefits for your well-being. We've put together more than two dozen prompts (beginning on page 88) to help you get started. They're designed to give even the busiest of us a few moments to reflect, renew and revitalize, so we can appreciate all of the amazing things that come with being a mom. ❧

Taking care of
yourself is crucial for
you to be the best
mom you can be.

CHAPTER

1

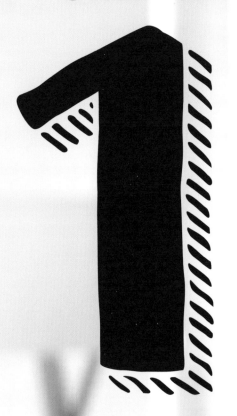

TAKING A PAUSE

WE NEED A BREAK NOW MORE THAN EVER—
AND THAT GOES DOUBLE FOR MOMS!
LEARN WHY EMBRACING MINDFUL HABITS
MAY BE JUST WHAT YOU NEED TO STAY SANE.

THE MAGIC OF MINDFULNESS

Trying to be more in the moment can be a tall order when you're coping with the many demands of motherhood—but it can make a big difference in your health, your mindset and even your parenting.

Like a lot of things in life—eating more fruits and veggies, exercising every day, getting to bed an hour earlier—I know mindfulness is good for me. But as a single mom of three kids—ages 12, 11 and 9—who is frantically juggling a full-time job along with remote school learning, the idea of going into a separate room and chanting "om" seems, well, downright daunting, and just a bit ludicrous. (Unless some deep breaths in the bathroom while my kids bang on the door and my dog howls just outside it count.)

But it turns out that practicing mindfulness may be easier than I thought. "It's more than being very present in the moment," reassures Bruce Rabin, MD, PhD, emeritus professor of preventative medicine at the University of Pittsburgh. "It's focusing on life as it's unfolding right in front of you, rather than letting your mind wander." In fact, he adds, research has consistently shown that mindful practices may help relieve stress, ease depression and anxiety, assist in weight loss and even reduce your risk of developing heart disease. And while mindfulness is always important, in these hectic, constantly changing times, it's more vital now than ever before. "The extra juggling all of us moms are doing right now makes it more important than ever to find ways to stay present," says Angela Ficken, LCSW, a social worker in Boston. "It's a helpful tool to help us manage when we feel out of control."

To practice mindfulness, don't view it as something that you need to schedule into your day—that will just stress you out even more, advises New York City wellness expert Tara Stiles, author of *Clean Mind, Clean Body: A 28-Day Plan for Physical,*

Time outside, either alone or with your family, helps boost your emotional well-being.

Give yourself a few minutes of "me" time to recharge and reconnect whenever you can find it. The dishes can wait!

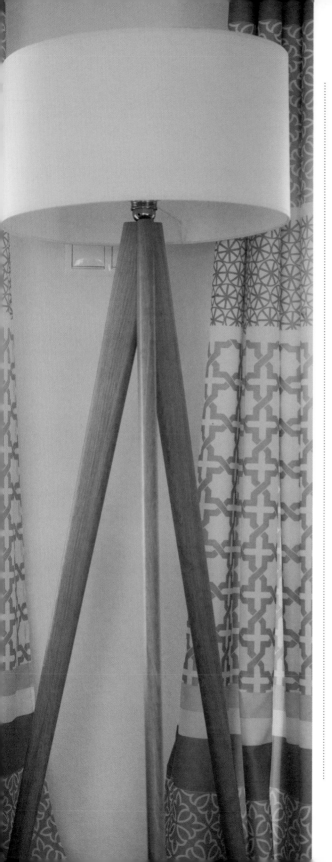

Mental, and Spiritual Self-Care. "Sure, we'd all love to take more bubble baths, but most of us can't set aside time for ourselves," she notes. Instead, try to find ways to connect with yourself, whether you're in the midst of homeschooling, cooking or a Zoom meeting for work. "When you adopt a more realistic view of mindfulness, you're more likely to use it, which in turn will allow you to better focus on everything you need to do," adds Stiles.

Consider these easy ways to help add some more mindful moments to your day:

SAVOR YOUR A.M. TIME

Wake up a few minutes earlier than usual and spend about 10 minutes using a meditation app such as Headspace, or try meditating without the app if you are comfortable doing so. "When you wake up and immediately look at your phone or start parenting, it can be an abrupt transition, which sets you up for a day of feeling overwhelmed and anxious," says Beth Tyson, a psychotherapist in Media, Pennsylvania. But if you start out your day doing something that's just for you, it helps set a positive tone for what lies ahead. "You go into parenting and responsibilities knowing you already contributed to your own well-being," adds Tyson.

MINDFULLY BRUSH YOUR TEETH

Even mundane daily tasks like brushing your teeth or washing the dishes can get a mindful makeover. "Instead of brushing your teeth thinking about your

REWIRE MINDFULNESS SO IT'S NOT A SEPARATE THING ON YOUR TO-DO LIST BY BRINGING IT INTO MORE EVERYDAY MOMENTS."

TARA STILES, WELLNESS EXPERT

> DONATE JUST A MINUTE OR EVEN 30 SECONDS TO YOURSELF SO YOU CAN REFUEL YOUR TANK AND HAVE MORE BANDWIDTH TO GIVE."
>
> ANGELA FICKEN, LCSW

to-do list, zero in on the scents of the toothpaste," advises Rebecca Leslie, PsyD, a psychologist in Atlanta. "Focus on what it feels like to brush your teeth, and bring all your attention to the present moment, engaging all of your senses."

DO SOME MIDMORNING JOURNALING

A study published in the *Journal of Happiness Studies* found that people who kept a gratitude journal for just two weeks reported better moods and less anxiety than those who did not write down their feelings. "Try to do 10 minutes of journaling affirmations, such as what you hope to achieve for the day and why you deserve this achievement," suggests Tyson. There are plenty of great options right in this book, starting on page 88!

PRACTICE BREATHING WITH YOUR KIDS

When your entire household is cranky and having a midafternoon meltdown, it's a good idea to do some easy breathing exercises to reset. "It's not the deep breathing that matters—it's the slow breathing that quells anxiety and balances our emotions," explains Tyson. Take a slow breath in to the count of four, hold it for one or two seconds, and then exhale longer than you inhaled for a count of six to eight. Repeat five times while visualizing your feelings and thoughts floating by on clouds above you. If you have small children, try this meditation move: Have your little one lie down with a favorite small stuffed animal on their tummy. Tell them to watch the toy rise and fall as they breathe in and out slowly.

TAKE A MINDFUL FAMILY WALK

"When we're in nature, time slows down and you can feel all the peacefulness around you," says Tyson. (A walk around your neighborhood counts!) While you are walking, encourage your kids to notice every step, the sound of trees blowing in the wind and cars in the distance, as well as the smell of the air. "To increase mindfulness, stay focused on sensory perceptions," adds Tyson. "Doing so keeps your brain in the 'here and now' or present moment." Or pick a cue that you notice on your walk as a trigger to pay attention.

"Choose to notice a particular thing, like a particular color of leaf, or a bicycle," adds Maya Frost, a mindfulness trainer in Portland, Oregon. Whenever you see that cue, notice it, take a deep breath, and tell yourself, "I'm paying attention." Then move on. "It might take all of 15 seconds, but it's enough to pull you out of your thoughts and into the present moment," says Frost.

And always remember, tomorrow is just another day. "It's important to remind yourself throughout the day that all we truly have is today," says Tyson. "The past is over and the future is yet to come. All you need to do is make it through today with peace." That can take the pressure off you thinking that as a mom you have to remain balanced and calm no matter what the universe throws at you. "Remembering that you only have to get it 'right' as a mom today puts things in perspective and makes it feel possible," adds Tyson.

As for me, I began practicing mindfulness where I know I'm guaranteed some privacy for even just a couple minutes: the bathroom. I run cold water on my wrist for 30 seconds while taking some deep breaths. I can feel myself visibly relax, and feel more grounded. These small slivers of mindfulness here and there over time can really add up, says Ficken. Personally, if it makes me feel less like the Tasmanian devil and more like a real mom when I'm with my kids, it's totally worth it. —*Hallie Levine*

SERENITY NOW!

Take a cue from some other women who have managed to find ways to stay centered and sane no matter what the day may throw at them.

→ **"I SET AN ALARM** to deep-breathe for one minute every hour on the hour, and I typically say, 'Girl you got this!' about 7,000 times a day when my kids lose it!"
—**Leslie Urbas,
Jacksonville, Florida**

→ **"WHENEVER I FEEL** overly stressed, I hold something meaningful to me that triggers positive memories, such as a picture, souvenir or piece of jewelry.

I meditate on those thoughts for five minutes, recalling every detail possible. It helps me center on what I truly value, and creates a renewed sense of deep gratitude."
—**Sabrina Hamilton,
Aurora, Colorado**

→ **"I'LL PAUSE BRIEFLY** just to take in a deep breath and feel my body relax. I also try to focus on pointing out beauty to my children—sunsets, the moon, pretty clouds, sounds

from nature, things like that. It helps us all slow down and remember what's most important in life."
—**September Burton,
Colorado Springs, Colorado**

→ **"I'VE TRAINED MY FAMILY** to recognize Mommy's 'coffee time' because they know they'll get the best version of me if I can linger over my steaming mug of calm."
—**Stacey Mitry,
Denver, Colorado**

Make your morning coffee a meditative experience by tuning in to all of your senses.

MANAGING MODERN
MOTHERHOOD

Multitasking has its place, but there are also times when only your undivided attention will do.

Guess what? It's impossible to have it all—
and that's OK. Instead, taking care of your needs
along with your family's will go a long way
toward making everyone happier.

Let's just say, hypothetically, that you are a writer working on a piece about finding "balance" in modern motherhood and you post queries in moms' groups looking for tips from the front lines. You might find your posts racking up kind—but clear—comments suggesting that you have the question all wrong, that there is no such thing as balance in modern motherhood—and presuming there is just adds yet another item to a to-do list that's already running off the page.

And then you'd call maternal mental health professionals, and they'd agree.

"Even asking the question alludes to this assumption that because people are feeling overwhelmed, there *is* something wrong," says Kate Kripke, LCSW, founder and CEO of the Postpartum Wellness Center in Boulder, Colorado. There is something wrong, she says—but it's not what moms are (or are not!) doing. Rather, it's more an issue of what we expect of moms and the insufficient resources we give them to do it. "We're trying to do it all," says Kripke, "but the system is not set up to help us—biologically, socially and psychologically—so we can't. And then we feel like there's something wrong with *us*. It's a recipe for disaster."

"I really think the word 'balance' is part of the problem," agrees Graeme Seabrook, a life coach who works with moms in Aurora, Colorado, "because it makes us think that balancing is something we should be able to do. It's kind of like if we all decided one day that Bigfoot is real, and everyone decided to go look for it. But we never find it, because there is no freaking Bigfoot."

Instead, says Seabrook, if we can all agree that finding balance is a myth, we can begin the more fruitful work of figuring out what it is we actually need to maintain some level of sanity in the madness of modern motherhood. Buh-bye, "balance."

Most of the moms and experts I interviewed for this piece see their lives operating in a cyclical way, with demands of motherhood, paid work, household and other obligations ebbing and flowing over time.

"Things got better for me when I realized 'balance' is not a point," shares Michelle Hiskey,

> **"**
> IT'S OK TO JUST BE
> GOOD ENOUGH—BECAUSE
> WHAT YOU CONSIDER TO BE
> YOUR MEDIOCRE SELF IS
> PROBABLY AMAZING."
>
> NITZIA LOGOTHETIS, FOUNDER,
> THE SELENI INSTITUTE

Whether you work outside the home or are a full-time caregiver, set realistic expectations for what you can achieve.

Want to be a good role model for your kids? Respect yourself as much as you do the rest of your family.

a writer and editor in Decatur, Georgia. "It's a range. Not everything is balanced at the same time." Hiskey, whose kids are almost out of the house, finally learned that, for her, the goal for motherhood was "the absence of chaos and a sense of fulfillment."

Great goal. But how do we get there?

FIGURE OUT WHAT YOU NEED

Seabrook began experiencing a better life as a working mom when she started constantly asking herself, "What is it I want and need in a moment?" In those times of typical family stress, like, for example, when her 3- and 5-year-old are "standing inches from each other, screaming in each other's faces," when

part of her "wants to snap," Seabrook says, she stops and asks herself, "What do I need right now?"

Sometimes the answer is that she needs to walk away, breathe deeply and calm down before she responds to whatever particular mayhem is unfolding. "It's OK to let them be mad at each other while I give myself a moment," adds Seabrook.

Equally important, she says, is figuring out what you need on a daily or weekly basis to feel grounded. Kripke asks moms to come up with "three things you know you need to feel mentally well." There are lots of options, including sleep, exercise, time outside or with friends, going to the movies, reading. It doesn't matter what your three are, but they

ADVICE FROM THE TRENCHES

We may have different backgrounds and obligations, but we all know the challenges that come with raising kids. Here's how other moms make it work.

→ PUT THE "CO" BACK IN COPARENT If you are raising your child with another human, then by all means, that person should be sharing the psychological and logistical burden of parenthood. "I ask my partner to do more/lead-parent more often so I can do my work," says Betsy Prueter, who's a mom of three in Atlanta and chief of staff at a nonprofit. "That's not some magic strategy, but so many things that women do in search of 'balance' sacrifice themselves, their work and their mental health. No one asks dads how they find balance!" That's a great place to start a conversation with your partner. What does he or she need to make parenthood more manageable, and how can you work together to make it a reality for both of you?

→ CREATE SPACE IN YOUR SCHEDULE This looks different for every family, but consider things like limiting how many activities each child can participate in, saying yes only to birthday parties of close friends, making time for outdoor play, taking advantage of after-school care and allowing kids to be bored so they learn to entertain themselves.

→ BUDGET FOR SELF-CARE Life coach Graeme Seabrook "runs away from home" during the week when hotel rates are lowest and makes use of online discounts. Look for Groupons to get deals on exercise classes or barter babysitting with another parent.

→ OUTSOURCE WHAT AND WHEN YOU CAN It's not an option for everyone—but if it's possible, build in budget items for outsourcing tasks that can tie you up, like lawn care, house cleaning, grocery shopping and laundry.

→ FIND SUPPORT Jesse Murdock says she's able to make single motherhood more workable because she's "spent a lot of time building my village. I've learned to reach out to ask for help when I need to (even though I've traditionally been someone who hates asking for help!)." She also found a local single-moms group, which she claims is "a lifesaver" in helping her find resources.

THE WORK/HOME SEESAW

Consider these tips from moms who are meeting the demands of a job outside the home in addition to motherhood.

→ **CONTROL WHAT YOU CAN** Many jobs don't allow much flexibility, but if yours does, consider what you can shift around to make things less hectic. "When scheduling meetings and providing my overall availability, I never provide Friday slots," says Brittney Grove, a mom in Atlanta. That gives her a day to catch up on emails or projects or to just run some errands.

Debbie Brooks found much-needed relief from the pressures of working motherhood when she heard "a female executive say she had to give permission for work to overlap home and for home to overlap work," says Brooks. "That's been huge for me." To help enforce those boundaries, Suzanne Brown, author of *Mompowerment: Insights From Successful Professional Part-Time Working Moms Who Balance Career and Family*, recommends "defining emergencies for your work colleagues, clients, manager and family so you all agree when you can infringe on those boundaries."

→ **CONSIDER MAKING A CHANGE** Many of the moms I surveyed said that everything changed for them when they were able to shift their work hours earlier (say, from 8 a.m. to 3:30 p.m.) or move to a part-time role, or work from home some days a week. This is not an option for many, but if your employer and your budget have any flexibility, put it on the table.

→ **TRY SOMETHING NEW** If your job requires travel or other hours that make being a mom extra difficult, start to snoop around for a similar position with less travel or better hours.

"become a nonpharmaceutical prescription for mental health," explains Kripke. "Just like if you are taking medicine to feel better or be well, you need to be doing these three things to feel well."

And they don't have to be big. One mom told me, "I read every night. It sounds like a little thing, but it is so important to get my head out of the household/work/parenting groove and immerse myself in something beyond the everyday."

Other activities moms shared with me: therapy, naps, alone time, creative projects, exercise, going to bed when the kids do, a weekly break from parenting (arranged with a partner, a babysitter or family pitching in), meditation, karaoke, dance and yoga.

MAKE IT NONNEGOTIABLE

"In general, as moms, we don't set boundaries around these nonnegotiable prescriptions," says Kripke. Instead, in moments of high stress and deadlines, they are the first things to go, giving us even less bandwidth to manage our increased demands.

To avoid this, Seabrook says, "I go on the calendar first." One of her nonnegotiables is two "running away from home" days every other month, when she finds an affordable local hotel and sleeps, watches movies and reads. If her husband or a business associate wants to schedule something at that time, "they can't," she says, because it's on the calendar. Her husband does the same. "If there's a scheduling conflict, it's the kids' stuff that has to bend," says Seabrook. "They may not be able to do three different after-school activities or go to every birthday party for every kid in the class. That's OK. It's not necessary."

She learned this lesson watching her mom "stress herself out" to shuttle Seabrook between things like Girl Scouts, piano and ballet. "She was not a happy person my entire time growing up—she was always super-stressed, always felt like she was running late." Seabrook made a conscious decision to "never bend on my emotional and physical health" as a mom. "One day, these kids are going to grow up and I am still going to have to live with my body and my emotional health for the rest of my life." So she protects it.

ALLOW YOURSELF TO BE HUMAN

"The very hard lesson I have learned—and have to keep relearning—is that you can't do it all well, all the time," says Sarah Bacon, a scientist and mom of two. Seabrook also gives herself "as much grace as humanly possible." Both women know there will be times when they can't be a great mom, but they can definitely be a good one. If Seabrook is heading into a particularly tough week, she gives herself a little preparatory talk on Sunday. "I tell myself, 'This week, I am not going to be the mom who listens to every single story and knows everything that's going on at school.'"

This is not rocket science. We all know this. But it takes some repetition for it sink in. As Megan

You don't have to be supermom to wear the "good parent" crown—just honor yourself.

WORKING MOMS ARE 18 PERCENT MORE STRESSED THAN OTHER PEOPLE—AND UP TO 40 PERCENT FOR THOSE WHO WORK FULL TIME WITH TWO KIDS."

INSTITUTE FOR SOCIAL AND ECONOMIC RESEARCH, UNIVERSITY OF ESSEX

Madison, an insurance adjuster and mom of two, told me, "I am starting to slowly—with my husband saying it over and over and with a therapist telling me—to not hold myself to unrealistic standards."

FOCUS ON WHAT YOU REALLY WANT

"All of us have a mom we want to be, and they are all different," says Seabrook. "That's not the perfect mom we judge ourselves against, but the mom we actually want to be in our gut. The better I treat myself, the closer I am to her." Seabrook likes to bake with her kids and have that be a rewarding and enjoyable experience for all of them. But she knows that, with two young children, she needs to "have the energy to deal with an utterly destroyed kitchen afterward. So I protect myself and my energy as much as possible so I can be the mom who can bake with them."

Seabrook encourages clients to think about the ways in which they value engaging with their kids, and then figure out what they need to be able to be present and enjoy *those* moments of parenting, letting the elements that are less important to you go. "If I tried to be the PTA mom, I couldn't be the baking mom," says Seabrook. "Stop being the mom everybody else expects you to be." Honoring the mom you want to be and taking care of the person you are is a great way to stay grounded. —*Kate Rope*

THE MYTH OF MULTITASKING

Experts say you'll actually get a lot more out of slowing down and focusing on one thing at a time. Here's why.

Taking time to prioritize one task at a time will actually increase your efficiency.

We've all been in those situations where we're expected to juggle multiple balls at once: You know, that scenario where you're on a work call while your kid is in the other room loudly calling for you to help her with her schoolwork while the dog simultaneously barfs on your best Oriental rug. But hey, you can multitask, no problem: It's just something that's naturally part of having two X chromosomes, right?

Actually, wrong. While we might think that our gender may make us an expert in this area, research suggests otherwise: Both women and men score equally poorly when they multitask, according to a 2019 study published in the medical journal *PLOS ONE*. "Your brain really can't do two cognitive tasks at the same time," explains Deanna Larson, MD, an internist in Omaha, Nebraska, who also serves as a "physician burnout" coach. "When you multitask, you are just switching tasks quickly. But every time you move from sending an email to talking to your kid, there's a stop/start process going on in your brain that costs you time. As a result, you work less efficiently and you're more likely to make mistakes. It also drains you emotionally and cognitively, so you're less likely to be at your best." Case in point:

A Stanford study published in the *Proceedings of the National Academy of Sciences* found that not only is multitasking less productive than focusing on one thing at a time, those regularly bombarded with several streams of electronic information (that's you checking your Twitter feed while on a Zoom call) have more trouble with focus, memory recall or actually switching tasks than those who don't.

One reason so many of us moms get sucked into the myth of multitasking, notes Larson, is because we feel obligated to be everything for everyone else—our kids, our boss, our spouse, even our parents. "We have to remember that we're important also and learn to say no," she stresses. Not to mention that our desire to multitask stems from a belief that we don't have time, "when in fact if we relax and release into the moment and focus on one thing at a time, we get everything done more efficiently and effectively, and we're much less stressed out than when we try to do both simultaneously," adds Jennifer Hamady, a performance coach and national board certified counselor in Washington, D.C.

HOW TO AVOID MULTITASKING

Of course, when your to-do list stretches for days and you've got multiple people issuing multiple demands, turning into a single-tasker is easier said than done. But you can make it more manageable.

● **PRIORITIZE, PRIORITIZE, PRIORITIZE**
A fundamental concept starts with realizing what is really essential and needs to be done versus what can wait for a later time, advises Elizabeth Jennings, OTD, an occupational therapist and life coach in Killeen, Texas. Start by creating a list around those items that can be planned for another day. "Prioritize things that need to happen immediately and knock those out," adds Larson. "Dishes and laundry can wait, but a deadline for work cannot."
● **DEVELOP A SCHEDULE** Consider creating a weekly schedule with 168 hours in a week versus 24 hours in a day to allow yourself to plan and shift tasks around without feeling the pressure of a 24-hour deadline or time crunch, says Jennings. One must-do to put on them every single day:

Plan out your week—not just your day—to find more windows of free time.

27

Add some mindfulness to
even basic household tasks.

proposal to write for a client, for example, set a timer to give yourself a mental break every 30 to 45 minutes by doing some sort of household chore. "This allows you to get up for 10 to 15 minutes to encourage blood flow through your body while washing dishes or loading the dishwasher, putting a load of laundry in or even going for a quick power walk," says Jennings. While you're doing this, be more intentional about what you're doing. "This will allow you to give your mind, body and soul what might be needed to complete the bigger task at hand without feeling so drained or physically and mentally burned-out," Jennings explains.

● **WORK ON SIMILAR TASKS TOGETHER**
It's easier to do more than one thing simultaneously if they are related, says Larson. This is because when you do one project or chore, your brain activates all the circuits and neurons related to it. When you switch to a new activity, your brain has to adjust. While the shift is quick, "it takes a toll on your memory and your focus," explains Larson. "As a result, it takes longer to do things, and you may not do as good of a job." This approach also allows you to see the big picture so that you can transfer knowledge back and forth between one task and another.

● **USE TECHNOLOGY TO HELP YOU MULTITASK**
Organize what you need to do in an app such as Trello. This will help prevent your brain from becoming overtaxed remembering everything you need to do. Set up automatic notifications, so you're not sidelined by unexpected deadlines. Another must-do: Turn off email and text alerts and only check them at scheduled times (for example, every one to two hours).

● **TAKE A BRAIN BREAK** Whether it's 30 minutes at lunchtime or two 15-minute breaks during the day, take some time to practice mindfulness, advises Hamady. This can be an outdoor walking meditation, sitting outdoors or simply closing your eyes and taking some deep breaths. "It's whatever works best to allow you to clear your head and give your brain a rest, so that it's recharged and ready when you do go back to work," she explains. 🌺

downtime. "I swear by this and encourage my clients to find hobbies that can take their mind off their responsibilities so that they can learn to love their lives again," says Larson.

● **BE FLEXIBLE** "If you are too tired and can't make a deadline, then some tasks may need to be planned strategically and intentionally for another day," says Jennings. "The key is for moms to be flexible and conscious enough to make those changes when needed." This will help to ensure that you're not burning the candle at both ends and expending all your energy by trying to complete too many things at one time.

WHEN YOU REALLY HAVE TO...

Despite all your best efforts, you may find that you do need to multitask at some point. And that's OK! Just keep in mind that there are ways to do this carefully, and which allow you to stay focused without becoming overwhelmed, says Larson.

● **SELECT YOUR TASKS STRATEGICALLY**
Pick something that requires less mental focus and energy that you can do quickly while working on a longer, more-complicated project. If you have a

CAN YOU MINDFULLY MULTITASK?

→ **MINDFULNESS AT ITS CORE** is about being present and in the moment—which isn't exactly compatible with doing a bunch of things simultaneously without spending much time thinking about any of them. "When multitasking, moms can sometimes go on 'autopilot' and give no thought to their own body or emotions," says life coach Elizabeth Jennings. "As a result, they're more likely to quickly fatigue or become exhausted from just going off pure fumes at times." The good news is, you can train your mind to focus better by incorporating short, succinct mindfulness exercises throughout your day. "Any sort of mindfulness break is key to improving your focus and overall attitude while completing tasks or getting work done," adds Jennings. "Remember moms, success is not just measured by checking tasks off a to-do list, but by the overall satisfaction of being able to show up completely and entirely as who you are in the task you are completing and the work you do."

→ **THE NEXT TIME** you find yourself wanting to multitask, bring the focus back to the immediate task at hand, advises Hamady. "Tell yourself that if you take on the immediate project with full awareness, you'll make more progress on it, and you can do the other task once it's done or you reach a natural break point," she says. Still distracted? Focus yourself by concentrating on your breath. (Take a slow breath in to the count of four, hold it for one to two seconds, and then exhale longer than you inhaled, for a count of six to eight.) Once the urge to multitask subsides, return to what you're doing. "Every busy mom knows that throughout her day, there will be multiple things constantly calling for her attention," explains Hamady. "This exercise allows your brain to fall into a more mindful state, which in turn will boost its attention and executive functioning."

You can boost clarity with just a few minutes of deep breathing.

EASY WAYS TO BE MINDFUL

Yoga and meditation are great, but other simple techniques also enable you to tune in to the moment.

Research has shown that people are happier when they're focused on the moment, whether it's the ripe peach they're eating or the song on the radio. But people's minds drift an average of 47 percent of the time, according to Harvard researcher Matt Killingsworth, PhD, who studied 15,000 individuals.

Certainly there are plenty of outside stimuli that distract us, such as daily tasks and interruptions (cellphones, email alerts, crying children). Plus, "stress triggers like bad news, a tone of voice or not feeling well can throw us for a loop," says Melissa Eisler, an ICF-certified executive and leadership coach and mindfulness facilitator in San Diego. Then there's the autopilot portions of our day, when our habits are so automatic, we think about anything but what we're doing. But it is possible to get better at paying attention to the here and now.

FORMAL VERSUS INFORMAL PRACTICES

Most forms of meditation, as well as movement practices like yoga or tai chi, are considered formal mindfulness practices, where we seek to "be in the present with nonjudgment," says New Jersey–based mindfulness coach Ryan Benz. "There is scientific evidence that at any age this practice can rewire the brain."

"When we are conscious and aware, we call the shots in how we want to be in our everyday environment," says Mary Beth Stern, a certified mindfulness-based stress reduction teacher and board-certified addiction counselor. "Otherwise, we're like a pinball machine, constantly reacting, reacting, reacting."

Informal mindfulness practices have the same stay-in-the-present-moment goals, but are more spontaneous and usually less time-consuming,

You'll reap mind-body benefits from any hike, but using your senses to experience the environment—a Japanese practice called *shinrin-yoku*—can have even more healing attributes.

Prevent cavities—
and take a minute
to tune in to the
present moment—
when brushing
your teeth.

yet just as effective. "Mindfulness can be done in such small increments," says Kayla Craft, a yoga teacher in Glens Falls, New York. "Just commit to something that takes two to five minutes."

There are many types of informal practices —try out several of these until you find one (or more) that seems to suit you.

COMMONPLACE ROUTINES

Anything rote falls into this category: driving to the grocery store, washing dishes, doing laundry or setting the table. The idea is to pay attention to all the ways your senses are being stimulated and tap into curiosity, gratitude, acceptance and wonder. Some examples:

- **BRUSHING YOUR TEETH** "Smell the toothpaste. Hear the sounds. Feel the bristles," says Stern. "This is a good place to train because it is a finite activity."
- **EATING** While zeroing in on the sensations of taste, Benz recommends "thinking about all of the people and resources it took to get food to your plate. Pay gratitude to that." Find more resources at thecenterformindfuleating.org.
- **WALKING** The difference between mindful walking and a regular stroll is that the focus is on *how* you're getting somewhere rather than *where* you're going (you can even do it in your backyard). Walk slowly, deliberately and "tune in to one step at a time, feeling your foot hit the earth," says Benz. "Some people even sync their breath and their steps."

OUTDOOR PURSUITS

Spending time in nature, really tuning in to its majesty and beauty, is one of the best ways to connect with the moment. Here are three of the best:
- **STARGAZING** Mark Westmoquette, the Saint Helena–based author of *Mindful Thoughts for Stargazers: Find Your Inner Universe*, says, "A beautiful night sky filled with twinkling stars can be very captivating, drawing us very naturally into an effortless awareness. Looking up, you can become fully present with your experience, noticing the vista, the gentle breeze on your skin, and the sounds of the night entering your ears. Worries and to-do lists quickly fade away."
- **FOREST BATHING** A Japanese practice known as *shinrin-yoku*, this simple practice can make a big difference, Craft says. There are so many sights, smells and sounds that can inspire wonder if you're paying attention as you walk in the woods, including the cyclical system of nature itself.
- **DOING YARD WORK** "People dread it, but I find it can be so serene and so quiet that it's something I look forward to," says Craft. It also works for indoor activities like dusting and making the bed.

QUICK FIXES

You don't have to do yoga or sit cross-legged on a cushion for hours to reap the benefits of the

CHOOSE AN ACTIVITY THAT YOU DO OFTEN THAT HAS A REPETITIVE RHYTHM. RHYTHMIC IS EASIER TO FOCUS ON BECAUSE IT'S PREDICTABLE AND CONSISTENT."

MELISSA EISLER, LEADERSHIP COACH

practice. Here are some quick ways to get centered in five minutes or less:
- **PRESS 'PAUSE'** This simple practice helps you to shift out of autopilot and take account of your thoughts and actions. "It's a crucial moment," Stern says. "You pause and you ask yourself where your attention is."

Whenever you realize your mind is wandering, Benz says, "to bring yourself back to the moment, take a deep, conscious breath. This sets off the parasympathetic nervous system in your brain, which is responsible for relaxation and calm."

It's also helpful when you're annoyed, like when you're stuck behind a slow driver. "When I find myself behind someone doing 10 mph in a 20 mph zone, I take the index finger of my right hand and push it into my left palm, like pressing a button," says Stern. This simple act reminds her to calm down and experience the moment without judgment.
- **GO OUTSIDE** Even if all you have is two minutes, step outdoors and feel the sun, look at the clouds or turn your face up to the rain.
- **CHECK IN WITH YOURSELF** Benz suggests setting an alert on your phone one or more times a day to remind yourself to take a breath and ask yourself: "How am I doing? What am I doing? Do I want to be doing this?" ❧

Even a few seconds of deep breathing is enough to calm the fight-or-flight response.

COPING WITH EVERYDAY CHALLENGES

Transferring the zen calm of your meditation session or yoga class to real life is harder than it seems.

It's easy enough to be mindful when things are calm and peaceful, like when you're taking a leisurely stroll through a garden and enjoying the sights, sounds and smells along the way. Unfortunately, most of life isn't a literal or figurative walk in the park. And who wants to be mindful while arguing with their spouse, racing to finish a work project or dealing with a toddler's temper tantrum?

You do. Really.

"Mindfulness is about living in the moment, learning how to show up and become an observer of yourself and life without judging it," says Stephanie Catalano, LCSW, author of *Mindful Makeover: Create the Life You Desire*. Catalano, who runs a mindfulness-based counseling service in Florida, adds that while becoming more mindful won't solve your problems, it will provide you with a "strong skill set to help you navigate every day of your life."

Jennifer Cohen Harper, MA, who trains children, teens and educators around the world in mindfulness via her NYC-based company, Little Flower Yoga, notes that pausing to notice what's happening during the most hectic moments can help you get "unstuck" and figure out how to move forward. "In order to know what you need [to feel better], you have to first know what's going on with you," she says. "Consciously checking in with your energy level and emotional state helps you do that."

There's no one right way to practice mindfulness, but here are some ideas on how you might increase self-awareness throughout a stressful day so you're better prepared to handle whatever life throws at you.

FIRST THING IN THE MORNING

As nice as it would be to wake up to birds chirping and sunlight gently streaming through the window, most of us don't have mornings like that. Instead, you're more apt to hear a blaring alarm clock that's soon followed by the pings of urgent text messages or the sounds of children squabbling. Some of that may be unavoidable, but you can take a few minutes to carve out a mindful moment.

"For me personally, I like to meditate and get clear on my intentions for the day," says Catalano.

If meditation's not your thing, that's perfectly OK; you don't have to meditate to be mindful (or vice versa). "Just get up a few minutes early, when the house is still quiet, and try to immerse yourself in something with all your senses."

It's fine to pick something you have to do anyway, like take a shower, and turn it into a mindful experience: Really tune in to how the hot water feels on your body, listen to the sound of the stream hitting the tiles, watch as the steam fogs up the glass and inhale deeply as you notice the aroma of your soap and shampoo. If you recently brushed your teeth, make a point of noticing the minty taste in your mouth. "Try to keep yourself in the present by asking, 'What do I see, feel, taste, smell and hear?'" says Catalano.

OBSESSING OVER THE "WHAT IFS?"

Whenever you feel overwhelmed to the point that it's paralyzing you, channel Princess Anna in *Frozen 2* and remember that all you have to do is the next right thing, suggests Cohen Harper. Whether you're reeling after a fight with your mother-in-law or stressed about your seemingly endless to-do list, "the point is that you don't have to figure everything out, just what's next," she explains. It's a useful concept for kids and adults alike who tend to get caught up in anxious cycles of rumination.

YOUR BOSS ASKS A QUESTION YOU WEREN'T PREPARED TO ANSWER

Don't freeze up or blurt out the first thing that comes to mind, advises Catalano. Instead, buy yourself the time you need: "I will get back to you on that" or "I don't know but I will find out" are acceptable responses.

TRYING TO DO TOO MUCH AT ONCE

Imagine a stop sign or red traffic light in front of you. "When I find myself multitasking or juggling too much and I start to stress about the laundry, emails or drifting to things that happened in the past, I notice that and return to the present moment," says Catalano.

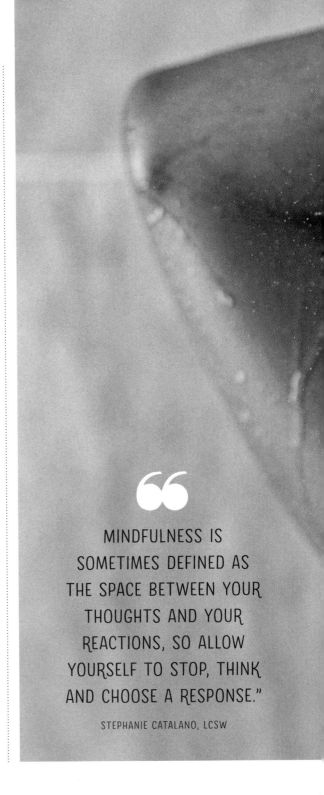

> **MINDFULNESS IS SOMETIMES DEFINED AS THE SPACE BETWEEN YOUR THOUGHTS AND YOUR REACTIONS, SO ALLOW YOURSELF TO STOP, THINK AND CHOOSE A RESPONSE."**
>
> STEPHANIE CATALANO, LCSW

Yes, a formal meditation practice is great, but acknowledging the simple pleasures of life can also help ease tension and make you more mindful.

HELPING KIDS BE MINDFUL

As with adults, children should be taught to practice mindfulness regularly, so that they have the tools in place when they really need them most—like being stressed-out at school. "You can't teach a drowning person to swim," says mindfulness expert Jennifer Cohen Harper. Here are a few ways to prepare your kids.

→ **TELL THEM TO DRAW THEIR BREATH** Tape a piece of paper to a wall. Tell kids to draw upward on it as they breathe in and downward as they breathe out. This is a good option for kids as young as 2 or 3; the goal is simply to get them used to noticing breathing patterns so they can learn to control them as they get older.

→ **TEACH THEM TO COUNT THEIR BREATHS** Kids 6 and up can practice breathing in while mentally counting "1, 2, 3," then out while counting "1, 2, 3, 4, 5, 6." The exhale should be longer than the inhale because it helps empty the lungs of deoxygenated air and triggers a calming response via the parasympathetic nervous system, Cohen Harper explains.

→ **URGE THEM TO LISTEN TO THEIR BODY** When you feel nervous, sad or upset, these emotions often trigger physical sensations like butterflies in your stomach or tense shoulders. "When kids don't understand those sensations, it makes them worse," says Cohen Harper. So instead of telling them to push those feelings and sensations away, encourage children to acknowledge what's happening and what they're feeling. "When they're able to notice the sensations that arise, negative emotions aren't so scary," she explains.

→ **MODEL MINDFUL BEHAVIOR** "If I'm having a hard time, my kids can see that," says Cohen Harper. "Instead of hiding it, I'll verbalize it and say, 'I'm getting really overwhelmed, so I'm going to sit for two minutes while breathing really slowly with one hand on my heart and one on my belly. I'll see how I feel after that.' It doesn't mean everything will be OK, but I'm sending a message to my mind that I'm safe right now and we can figure it out."

Yoga enhances kids' flexibility, strength and coordination and it helps them feel more relaxed.

Reaching out to a friend can help you feel more connected and less out of control.

If you can't let go of all the clutter in your mind, try jotting down a list of things to worry about later at a specific time. You might feel calmer knowing that you're not ignoring your clogged email inbox; it just doesn't deserve your attention at this moment.

BRACING YOURSELF FOR RELATIVES WHO TEND TO PUSH YOUR BUTTONS

As difficult as it might sound, try to embrace your inner child and go in with a blank slate—which means mentally erasing any expectations you have about how the interaction is likely to go. "Ask yourself, 'How can I show up as if I'm experiencing it for the first time?'" says Catalano. "Try to go in with a sense of openness, curiosity and imagination."

WHEN YOU CAN'T QUIET YOUR RACING MIND

Try doing a simple progressive muscle-relaxation exercise: Mentally scan each body part, from the top of your head all the way down to your toes. As you picture each part, tense and release the muscles surrounding it. You can simply notice how each part feels as you breathe deeply, or you can spend an extra moment appreciating what it did for you earlier that day—which is what Cohen Harper advises children do in her new kids' book, *Thank You Body, Thank You Heart: A Gratitude and Self-Compassion Practice for Bedtime*. No matter your age, "exercising the 'gratitude muscle' helps reduce anxiety and foster a stronger connection with your own body," she says. 🌺

The average person takes anywhere from 17,000 to 23,000 breaths a day.

BREATHING LESSONS

Learning to exhale (and inhale)
strategically can lower stress
and anxiety, reduce blood pressure
and help you think more clearly.

I f you can read this sentence, you know how to breathe. Even though you probably don't think much about your breathing, you should. Breathing the right way has been scientifically proven to help lower the risk of heart disease and boost overall physical and psychological health.

And while you pretty much came out of the womb knowing how to breathe, learning a few techniques is a potent way to reduce fatigue and anxiety and ensure that you stay on top of your game, even when life starts to get stressful, says Rachel Tomlinson, PhD, a psychologist in Perth, Australia.

ANATOMY OF A BREATH

Ready for a quick breathing tutorial? When you breathe in, your diaphragm—the main muscle used for breathing—contracts and moves downward, allowing your lungs to expand into your chest. Meanwhile, the muscles between your ribs contract to pull your rib cage upward and outward, giving your chest cavity more space. As your lungs expand, air passes through your nose or your mouth, down your windpipe and deep into the air sacs of your lungs. This allows the oxygen you inhaled to pass into your bloodstream, where it's then transported to all the cells of your body, explains Diane Malaspina, PhD, a yoga medicine therapeutic specialist in Virginia Beach, Virginia.

When you breathe out, your diaphragm and rib muscles relax, decreasing the space in your chest cavity. As it gets smaller, your lungs deflate like a balloon, allowing carbon dioxide–rich air to flow out of your nose or mouth.

WHY YOU NEED TO DO IT CORRECTLY

Breathing isn't as easy as it seems. The two most important things are to breathe through your nose, and to engage your diaphragm, aka belly breathing. "The nose filters and humidifies your breath, and nose-breathing paces your breath to provide your lungs enough time to extract the maximum amount of oxygen and energy from each breath," explains Malaspina. When you breathe deeply through your belly, it also massages your internal organs, which in turn improves digestion and elimination, she adds. It helps your ticker, too: It slows your heart rate and reduces blood pressure, and it also lowers levels of stress hormones such as adrenaline and cortisol that raise your risk of heart disease. Just five minutes of deep-breathing exercises lowered heart rate and blood pressure, according to a 2011 study published in the *International Journal of Yoga Therapy*.

It has psychological benefits as well. "The deeper and longer your breathing, the more oxygen you can take in and the more relaxed and clear-minded you become," explains Mendy Dubov, managing partner of Jump Agency, a peak-performance training company in Maitland, Florida. A 2017 study published

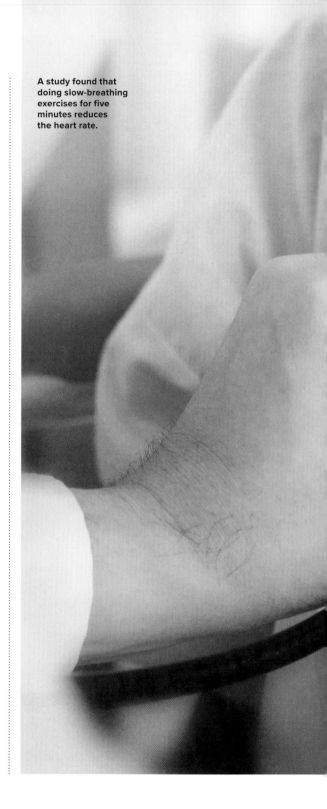

A study found that doing slow-breathing exercises for five minutes reduces the heart rate.

> **"**
> BECAUSE THE
> BREATH IS ALWAYS
> WITH US, IT CAN
> BE USED TO CULTIVATE
> MINDFULNESS AT
> ANY TIME."
>
> RACHEL TOMLINSON, PHD

in the journal *Frontiers in Psychology* found that people who received 20 deep-breathing training sessions over an eight-week period not only had lower cortisol levels but also reported better attention and focus.

HOW BREATHING IMPACTS MINDFULNESS

Breathing is one of the best weapons in your mindfulness toolbox because you can do it anywhere, anytime—there's no yoga mat or self-help book required. "Whether in the car, walking down the street or sitting in a meeting, bringing awareness to the breath draws our attention back to this one moment," Tomlinson points out. Since it gives you something specific to focus on—inhaling and exhaling—when your mind starts to wander, you don't get distracted by worries or other negative emotions.

HOW TO BREATHE BETTER

There are several belly-breathing exercises you can easily do at home. The most basic one is to simply sit in a chair, your knees bent and your shoulders, head and neck relaxed. Now place one hand on your upper chest and the other just below your rib cage, so you can feel your diaphragm move as you breathe. Breathe in slowly through your nose, feeling your stomach move against your hand. Now tighten your stomach muscles and exhale through your lips,

THE DEEPER AND LONGER YOUR BREATHING...THE MORE OXYGEN YOU CAN TAKE IN AND THE MORE RELAXED AND CLEAR-MINDED YOU BECOME."

MENDY DUBOV, PERFORMANCE TRAINING EXPERT

keeping the hand on your upper chest as still as possible. Practice this four to five times a day for five minutes at a time; it will help relieve shortness of breath and make every breath more effective. A 2010 study published in the *Journal of Alternative and Complementary Medicine* found that women who practiced this type of slow abdominal breathing reduced their body's fight-or-flight response and stimulated the activity of their vagus nerve, another important component of stress reduction.

Once you've mastered this, you can move on to other techniques like even breathing, which helps you cultivate a sense of balance, says Malaspina. Inhale slowly through your nose to a count of four, pause, then exhale slowly to a count of four. Repeat for several rounds. You can further lower stress and anxiety by extending the inhale: Breathe in for a count of six, then exhale for a count of four.

Alternate-nostril breathing is another advanced technique that's used in yoga to balance the nervous system, adds Malaspina. This technique—where you rotate inhaling through one nostril and exhaling through the other—is thought to harmonize the two hemispheres of the brain and balance your physical, mental and emotional well-being. A 2013 study in the Journal of Clinical and Diagnostic Research found that people who practiced alternate-nostril breathing lowered their perceived stress levels. Here's how to do it:

1 Lift your right hand to your face so that your pointer and middle fingers rest between your eyebrows.

2 Close your eyes and inhale and exhale deeply through your nose.

3 Close your right nostril with your right thumb while inhaling through your left nostril.

4 Close your left nostril with your ring finger so both nostrils are held closed for a moment, then open your right nostril and exhale slowly through your right side.

5 Inhale through your right nostril, then hold both nostrils closed with your ring finger and thumb.

6 Open your left nostril and exhale slowly through your left side. Repeat five to 10 times. ❧

TAKE A BREATHER

De-stress on the spot with these techniques.

Whether you're in the school carpool line, on a work conference call from hell or having an intense conversation with your partner, these three exercises, courtesy of Rachel Tomlinson, PhD, will keep you centered.

→ **PURSED-LIP BREATHING** Relax your neck and drop your shoulders. Keep your mouth closed and inhale slowly through your nose for five seconds. Purse your lips as if you are about to whistle. Exhale slowly and blow air through your pursed lips for five seconds. Repeat five times.

→ **EQUAL BREATHING** Breathe in and out through your nose until you find a breath length that feels comfortable (not too long or short). During each inhale and exhale, count to make sure the in and out breaths are even. You might add in a slight pause after each inhale or exhale if this feels comfortable. Continue for five minutes.

→ **BUBBLE BREATHING** Breathe in slowly through the nose (for five) and out through the mouth (for five), as if you are blowing bubbles. The slower you breathe, the bigger the bubbles. Try for at least 10 "bubble breaths."

Learn some calming breathing techniques so you'll be ready when stress kicks into high gear.

People who express their appreciation for the good things in their lives report fewer symptoms of physical illness, according to a 2017 report in *The Review of Communication*.

THE POWER OF
APPRECIATION

Gratitude is one of the most potent tools in your mindfulness arsenal.

t's difficult to feel grateful when you're stuck in rush-hour traffic, you spilled your coffee all over your brand-new handbag and you have to figure out how you're going to finish your latest work project in time to make it to one of your kids' soccer games. When you're in this stressed-out, frazzled mindset, it's hard to remember to take some deep breaths and just be thankful that you're alive.

But there are many important reasons why you should. "If a person can adopt a grateful orientation toward life, recognizing sources of goodness, they will see very real physical and mental benefits," explains Robert Emmons, PhD, a professor of psychology at the University of California, Davis. His own research has found that people who regularly practice gratitude experience more positive emotions, feel more alert, are aware of more joy and pleasure, get more sleep—and even suffer from fewer aches and pains than those who don't. "Gratitude allows us to celebrate the present, and it magnifies positive emotions," he says. It also blocks toxic, negative emotions, such as jealousy and bitterness, which can destroy our happiness.

Grateful people also appear to be more resilient in the face of stress and more serious trauma. "It helps us find balance and more harmony with what we have and who we are already, helping us get a reality check," explains Bruce Rabin, MD, PhD, professor emeritus of preventive medicine at the University of Pittsburgh. As a result, people who practice gratitude tend to be able to bounce back more quickly.

WHY GRATITUDE IS GOOD FOR YOU

Here's why gratitude will make you a happier, healthier person, says Rabin:

● **IT BOOSTS YOUR MOOD** When researchers rated the levels of gratitude among people with existing heart disease, they found that those with higher gratitude scores reported better moods and quality sleep, and they had fewer markers of inflammation in their body (like C-reactive protein), according to a 2015 University of California, San Diego study.

● **IT IMPROVES YOUR SLEEP** A 2009 University of Manchester study of 400 adults—40 percent of whom had some sort of sleep disorder—found that people who reported feelings of gratitude at bedtime fell asleep faster and had better quality sleep than those who didn't.

● **IT HELPS YOU MAKE NEW FRIENDS** Thanking a new acquaintance makes them more likely to warm up to you and to seek a more personal relationship, according to a 2015 study published in the journal *Emotion*. This in turn can help relieve stress, explains Rabin.

● **IT MOTIVATES YOU TO TAKE BETTER CARE OF YOURSELF** A 2013 Swiss study published in *Personality and Individual Differences* found that grateful people not only experience fewer aches and pains, they also are more proactive about their health, including exercising frequently and making sure they stay on top of regular checkups.

HOW TO INCORPORATE GRATITUDE INTO YOUR DAY-TO-DAY LIFE

For some people, a 20-minute gratitude daily meditation is their practice of choice, while for

" WHEN WE APPRECIATE THE VALUE OF SOMETHING, WE EXTRACT MORE BENEFITS FROM IT."

ROBERT EMMONS, PHD

Tell your colleagues how much you appreciate them: Portland State University researchers found that being thanked at work predicted better sleep, fewer headaches and a healthier diet.

49

In addition to taking time to savor every bite, mindful eating can also mean sending out some gratitude for everything that went in to making your meal.

others, it simply means practicing mindfulness in a stressful situation. "When you're in an anxious moment—for example, up against a deadline or stuck in traffic—it helps to just stop, take a few deep breaths and take a look at everything going on around you, while letting your emotions flow through you at the same time," says Rabin. Try incorporating these five tips into your life to establish a gratitude practice:

● **EXPRESS GRATITUDE TO OTHERS** See someone doing a good job at work? Tell them. When researchers looked at nurses—a career that has a high level of burnout—they found that those who were thanked more often at work had better sleep, fewer headaches and healthier eating habits than those who didn't receive acknowledgment of their efforts, according to a March 2019 study published in the *Journal of Positive Psychology*. They're also more likely to return the favor, leading to a virtuous cycle of appreciation that can only improve your own mood and health, says Rabin.

● **VOLUNTEER** Altruism inspires gratitude because it puts your own issues in perspective, says Gail Saltz, MD, clinical associate professor of psychiatry at Weill-Cornell Medical College. Giving to others not only makes you feel good, but it also makes you more grateful for what you do have in your life. If you don't have time to volunteer, just make more efforts to do good deeds, like helping an elderly neighbor grocery-shop, or writing a check to a favorite charity.

● **PRACTICE MINDFUL EATING** A great place to focus on gratitude is at mealtime, says Susan Albers, PsyD, a psychologist at the Cleveland Clinic and author of *Hanger Management: Master Your Hunger and Improve Your Mood, Mind, and Relationships*. If you're eating with others, share your gratitude for a few moments with friends or family before digging in. Since that first bite is the most flavorful, take the time to savor your food and be grateful for how it smells and how it feels in your mouth, says Albers. You'll not only inspire thankfulness, you'll end up eating less because you'll be more satisfied.

● **FOCUS ON INTENTIONS** When something good happens, think about how someone else brought that goodness into your life, and what they may have given up to do so, says Joyce Mikal-Flynn, EdD, FNP, MSN, a professor in the school of nursing at Sacramento State University in California. It can be something as simple as another driver letting you into their lane. These little gestures can go a long way toward cultivating an "attitude of gratitude," explains Mikal-Flynn.

● **COUNTER COMPLAINING** Complaining is easy to do, and oftentimes there's a good reason for it. But sometimes it's also a way to get stuck, says Rabin. Nip it in the bud by carrying around an index card on which you've written down some of your most frequent grumbles. Then flip it over and write a gratitude statement on the back. (For example, on one side write, "I hate grocery shopping" and then on the other side write, "But it allows me to eat dinner and spend time with my loving family, which I'm thankful for.") As time goes by, you'll eventually find that any time a complaint bubbles up, your brain will automatically focus on the positive. ✿

5 GRATITUDE PRACTICES YOU CAN DO IN 10 MINUTES OR LESS

→ **30 SECONDS** Thank a loved one. Each day, someone in your family—your spouse, your kids, even your four-legged fur babies—does something to make your life better. Take a moment to give them a hug and acknowledge what they did.

→ **ONE MINUTE** Jot down three things you're appreciative of. You can write them on a whiteboard or on pieces of paper that you stuff into a gratitude jar. Then whenever you feel down or like you're about to complain, look at the board or notes for a quick gratitude pick-me-up.

→ **TWO MINUTES** Write a thank-you note. They take only a couple of minutes to pen, but they can inspire intense feelings of gratitude in both the writer and the recipient, according to a 2018 study published in *Psychological Science*.

→ **FIVE MINUTES** Keep a gratitude journal. There's no need to write in it more than once a week:

Research done at the University of California, Riverside, found that people who wrote in their gratitude journals once a week for six weeks reported boosts in happiness afterward; people who wrote three times per week didn't.

→ **FIVE TO 10 MINUTES** Pray. Gratitude is often considered the most powerful form of prayer, says Robert Emmons, PhD, because through it, people recognize the ultimate source of all they are and all they will ever be.

SAYING YES TO AFFIRMATIONS

Scientists have discovered that what you say is often what you end up doing.

If you watched *Saturday Night Live* in the '90s, you might very well roll your eyes whenever self-affirmations are mentioned. After all, how can you take seriously something that was mocked so thoroughly by Al Franken's Stuart Smalley character, who regularly gazed in a mirror while earnestly repeating his signature lines like, "I'm good enough, I'm smart enough, and doggone it, people like me!"

But despite being ripe for parody, scientists have discovered affirmations do work. In a 2013 study published in *PLOS ONE,* a group of 80 stressed-out college students were asked to list 11 things—like politics, friends, family, music, religion—in order of importance. Half were told to write an essay about why their No. 1 value mattered so much to them personally; the other half wrote about one of their least-rated values and why it might be important to other people. Then they all took a series of tests that measured their problem-solving abilities. The students in the first group, who completed the self-affirmation—i.e., those who wrote about

something they personally valued—scored higher than those who had written about something they didn't particularly care about. It was as if the self-affirmation erased the stress—in fact, the first group scored as well as another group of test-takers who reported having low stress levels.

WHAT IS SELF-AFFIRMATION ANYWAY?

"Self-affirmation is more than the classic 'I am good' mantra," says Janine M. Dutcher, PhD, a research scientist in the department of psychology at Carnegie Mellon University in Pittsburgh. It is the process of thinking or writing about our core values. "As humans, we are motivated to see ourselves as decent and capable." Self-affirmation is when we remind ourselves that we possess those positive qualities that are important to us.

HOW IT WORKS

Self-affirmation theory, first popularized in the 1980s, contends that if we reflect on values that are personally relevant to us, we're less likely to get

"If you really think small, your world will be small. If you think big, your world will be big," novelist Paulo Coelho said on Oprah Winfrey's *SuperSoul Conversations*.

53

DEVELOPING AN AFFIRMATIONS ROUTINE

Try these techniques to empower yourself.

There are no hard rules about how to practice self-affirmation: You can speak affirmations out loud, repeat them silently in your head or journal them. There are books and apps devoted to daily affirmations. You can even make art with them. "The one thing that's mandatory is that you're consistent and your heart is in it," says author Jennifer Williamson. "You have to believe what you're affirming, so choose ones that speak to you. This might mean you're inspired by certain affirmations that others wrote, and then adjust them according to your personality, beliefs and life." Start with these tips:

→ **PICK YOUR PRONOUNS** Instead of using "I," use your own name. Admittedly, it might feel strange to refer to yourself in the third person, but it can be even more helpful than an "I am" statement. Here's why: "By creating distance from yourself with your language, you can be more rational and less emotional about the pronouns you use to describe yourself," says Williamson. "So, instead of saying, 'Jen, you idiot!' I might substitute that unhelpful phrase with a more helpful one, like 'It's OK to be human, Jen.'"

→ **USE THE PRESENT TENSE** "I am in a healthy relationship" or "I can have a strong and healthy relationship" is more powerful than "I will be in a healthy relationship one day." Explains Williamson, "Even if you're not in a romantic relationship right now, you can start working on having a healthy relationship with yourself. Start where you are and work from there. 'I will' or 'I am going to' statements keep what you want in the future. Find creative ways to bring what you want into the present by using phrases like: 'I am learning how to...' or 'I am worthy of having....'"

→ **BELIEVE WHAT YOU'RE AFFIRMING** Your words are powerful—if you mean them. "If an affirmation is too far from your current belief, select another, or adjust it," says Williamson. "You can incorporate the word 'willing' or 'learning' to make it more fitting. For example: 'I am willing to believe....' For any affirmation to work, it has to be true for you; you have to believe what you're saying."

→ **BE PATIENT** If you encounter resistance, simply notice it. "Resistance to something new is natural. Give yourself compassion, be patient and give the new affirmation space to grow," says Williamson. "It's all a practice."

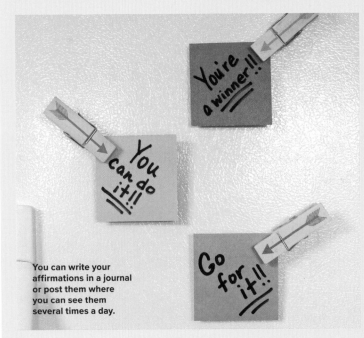

You can write your affirmations in a journal or post them where you can see them several times a day.

Follow through on your affirmations with positive actions, whether it's starting a yoga practice or volunteering.

upset or react defensively when we're confronted with information—such as stressful questions on a test or admonitions about our health—that contradicts the way we see ourselves.

"Affirmations are used to restructure our thought patterns and reprogram the subconscious mind," says Jennifer Williamson, the Spencer, Massachusetts-based author of *Morning Affirmations* and *Sleep Affirmations* and founder of healingbrave.com. "What we believe about ourselves on a subconscious level is a powerful thing. It shapes our behaviors, relationships and how we experience the world and our place in it. When you're using self-affirmations, you're essentially learning how to think differently about yourself."

Say, for instance, your mind chatter tends toward the negative: Your closest friends are more successful; your co-workers don't appreciate your strengths; you'll never find your soul mate. There's a self-fulfilling prophecy involved in negative thinking, but even knowing that doesn't make

it easy to stop. Try taking one negative thought at a time and replacing it with a positive one. Or "practice creating your own self-affirmations by identifying the thoughts you already think all the time, and find new ways to word them using gentler, more neutral language," says Williamson. "For instance, instead of looking in the mirror and saying 'I'm ugly' or 'I'm fat,' you could transition to 'I'm round here,' or 'I respect what my body has been through' or 'I'm excited to see how my healthy choices affect this area of my body.'"

Something else to keep in mind: "Whether or not we use affirmations intentionally, we're always affirming something," says Williamson. "Every time you think a certain way about yourself, you're affirming who you are. You could think that 'I'm not smart enough' or 'I'm going to figure this out'—both are affirmations, but one empowers you to keep going, and one makes you feel incapable of handling what life throws at you." ❧

MINDFULNESS IN MOTION

Enhance your overall well-being with practices that emphasize the brain-body connection, including yoga, Pilates and meditation.

There's more to a fit body than flat abs and toned arms. It's also about a clear, centered headspace that enables you to rise to any challenge that comes your way, which—as a mom—could be almost anything! And that's where mind-body practices—including yoga, Pilates and meditation—come in. Combining movement with mental focus and breath control helps increase calmness and improve psychological balance. Mind-body practices can boost your health and well-being in ways that mere physical exercise fails to do.

At first glance, these modalities seem similar: All are low-impact and accessible. All are rooted in the concept of staying present and tuning in to your body. And all feature specific breathing methods designed to calm the mind. But while there is crossover, the origins and approaches are different. Not sure which is for you? We asked experts for the lowdown on each, and share tips to help you get started.

Crazy day at the office or at home? Meditating or practicing yoga or Pilates can help you chill out.

YOGA

Dating back 5,000 years in India, yoga is a holistic discipline aimed at uniting mind, body and spirit. A variety of texts, traditions and teachers helped to shape the practice, which was introduced in the West in the late 19th century. With an estimated 800 different styles available—from ashtanga to yin, with Bikram, Iyengar and kundalini in between—there's a class for everyone. Today there are upward of 36 million practitioners in the U.S.

While often associated with stretching and exercise, yoga is more of a way of life than it is a workout. "The asanas, or physical postures, are just one of eight foundational principles of yoga, which also include breathing, meditation and attitudes toward the environment and ourselves," explains Jo-anne Lee, a New York City–based yoga and Pilates instructor and martial artist. Traditionally, the purpose of doing the poses was to prepare the body to sit for long periods of time in meditation.

"Yoga classes tend to begin with an intention to focus on the present moment," Lee says. "We do this by bringing the attention to the breath and how it resonates in the body." Conscious breathing powers down the sympathetic nervous system—your fight-or-flight response—and powers up the parasympathetic system, which calms the body and brain.

A typical yoga class can include a series of standing and seated poses, such as twists, forward bends and backbends, all designed to open up the body and release tension. "The purpose of holding poses for a certain number of breaths allows you to refine your alignment, and then move consciously to the next," says Christine Gagen, a yoga and Pilates instructor in Greenport, New York, and Miami.

Class is likely to wrap up with savasana, also known as "corpse pose," where you'll lie on your back with your eyes closed and simply relax. "It symbolizes the letting-go of effort, the releasing of everything you've worked toward," Lee says.

STRIKE A POSE

New to yoga? Try these easy-to-master moves at home.

⬆**MOUNTAIN POSE** Start by standing with your feet together. Press down through all 10 toes and bring your arms next to your thighs. Engage your quads to lift your kneecaps. Draw your abs in and up as you lift your chest and press the tops of the shoulders down. Imagine a string drawing the crown of the head up to the ceiling and breathe deeply into the torso. Stay here for five breaths.

⬆**DOWNWARD-FACING DOG** Starting on all fours, press your hands firmly into the floor, tuck your toes and lift your hips up and back to create a triangle shape with your body. Your feet should be parallel, with the heels pressing toward the floor. Let your head hang between your arms and stay here for five breaths.

Try to avoid competing in yoga class. Instead, focus on compassion and self-love—or just your breathing.

↑**TREE POSE** From a standing position, slowly press the sole of one foot into the inner thigh of the opposite leg. (If this is too difficult, place it alongside your ankle or calf.) Focus your gaze on a fixed point. Once you feel steady, press your palms together in front of your chest. Stay here for five breaths, then switch legs.

↑**BRIDGE POSE** Lie on your back and place your feet hip-width apart. Press firmly into your feet and lift your butt up off the mat. Interlace your hands together and press them down to the floor as you open up your chest even more, or keep your arms straight and press down. Stay here for eight to 10 breaths, then lower your hips down and repeat twice more.

↑**EXTENDED CHILD'S POSE** Come into a kneeling tabletop position with your big toes together, then sit back on your heels. Lengthen your spine up through the crown of your head. On an exhalation, bow forward, draping your torso over your thighs. Allow your forehead to rest on the floor with your arms extended in front of you. Close your eyes and stay here for eight breaths.

OM ON DEMAND

Got space for a mat—and a good Wi-Fi connection? Get your yoga fix
in the comfort of your own home with one of these class-streaming sites.

→ **GLO** This site offers more than 300 classes, including more than a dozen programs for newbies. Taught by some of the country's best instructors, classes range from five to 90 minutes. You can choose from super-physical ones or those that have a more spiritual or meditative bent. As a member, you'll also have access to lectures and workshops by yoga scholars. (*$18/month; glo.com*)

→ **YOGA ANYTIME** Practice self-care alongside 100-plus yoga pros who lead practices and meditations in a variety of styles, levels and durations, including live classes. With a subscription, you'll get unlimited access to the library of 2,900 yoga and meditation videos, as well as "yoga shows" like *30-Minute Yoga Flows* and *The Happy Back*. (*$18/month; yogaanytime.com*)

→ **YOGIAPPROVED** The wallet-friendly site streams a fun variety of yoga classes, as well as programs designed to expand your practice and build skills, from increasing flexibility to partner yoga. Download the YA Classes iOS app to take your practice to go. Need more incentive? A food-producing tree will be planted for every class you take. (*$14/month; yogiapproved.com*)

Home-based yogis say that having a designated space to practice is key.

Props are used in Pilates mat classes to give you an assist or to make exercises more challenging.

"It's there for your body to rest and receive the full effects of your practice."

And those effects are considerable. Some styles are more physically challenging than others, but all yoga poses are designed to tone, strengthen and align the body, increase flexibility of the muscles and joints, and improve balance. A growing body of research finds yoga can benefit people with chronic health conditions, ranging from back pain and high blood pressure to arthritis and asthma.

The mental and emotional perks are no less impressive: Incorporating yoga into your regimen has been shown to be an effective way to manage stress, ease anxiety and depression, and improve mood. One British study found subjects experienced an uptick in energy and self-esteem after striking yoga poses for just two minutes. The brain benefits, too: In a study in the *Journal of Physical Activity and*

Health, just 20 minutes improved participants' ability to quickly and accurately process information.

While you can get the basics from streaming classes (see sidebar, left), it's best to first learn from a certified yoga instructor, who can observe your form and make sure you're getting the most from every pose. Shop around until you find a beginner's class in a style that's suited to your personality and goals.

PILATES

Pilates is an exercise system featuring controlled, targeted strength moves and a focus on body awareness and the breath. Initially known as Contrology, it was created by Joseph Pilates in the 1910s as a rehabilitation program for World War I soldiers. Exercise enthusiasts and dancers soon became fans of the workout's emphasis on stability, flexibility and posture.

" YOGA...CAN IMPROVE
SYMPTOMS OF DEPRESSION AND
ANXIETY IN BOTH THE SHORT
TERM [WITH EACH SESSION]
AS WELL AS CUMULATIVELY...
OVER THREE MONTHS."

2019 BOSTON UNIVERSITY SCHOOL OF MEDICINE STUDY

Unlike yoga, which targets the whole body, Pilates classes center around stabilizing and strengthening the "powerhouse," or core muscles. "Pilates builds a suit of armor from within," says Julie Erickson, founder/owner of Endurance Pilates and Yoga Studio in Boston and NYC. "It teaches your body to engage the interior muscles, which brings you into better alignment and helps you move more efficiently."

Working against resistance is essential to the 500 Pilates exercises. This can be accomplished in a mat class, where you support your own body weight, or on a specialized piece of equipment like the Reformer, which has pulleys, straps and springs to make those muscles contract. As with other Pilates-specific apparatus—like the Cadillac, the Wunda Chair, the High Chair and the Barrel—Reformers allow for hundreds of exercises that work both small postural and large moving muscles simultaneously.

Classic Pilates classes usually follow a set sequence of standard movements, such as the Hundred and the One-Leg Circle. "Certain exercises are very close to the things we do in yoga," Erickson says. Open Leg Balance, for example, closely resembles yoga's navasana (boat pose), while the Pilates Roll Over is similar to halasana, or plough pose.

But while yoga requires moving from one static posture to the next, this workout involves "flowing" through a series of exercises. "In Pilates there is constant movement," says Linda Wirtz, a senior Pilates and yoga instructor at Bull Dawg Training in Arlington, Virginia. "The flow and repetitive nature of the workout creates grace and ease of movement, while building strength and stamina."

Breathing, while emphasized, may differ as well. "In Pilates, you tend to exhale through the mouth, as a conscious way of connecting with your pelvic floor and deeper abdominals," Lee says.

Pilates work is often incorporated in conventional therapies to facilitate healing and ward off future injury. "It aids in the alignment of the spine and pelvis and corrects muscular imbalances, while promoting good posture and agility," Wirtz says. But the benefits go beyond the physical. Studies find that regular practitioners sleep better and have lower stress levels. "Pilates requires good concentration of your body and breath with a deep focus," she explains. "So much of our stress is not getting those nice full breaths and clearing the lungs."

As with yoga, it's best to start with a beginner class. Whether you're interested in a mat class or one using the Reformer or other equipment, seek out a certified Pilates instructor (they'll have the initials PMA or NPCT after their name).

MEDITATION

A component of a well-rounded yoga practice, mindfulness meditation has been practiced in East and Southeast Asia since the Buddha began teaching it 2,600 years ago. Developed as a tool for achieving clarity and peace of mind, it involves taming the endless stream of thoughts floating in your head and freeing yourself of self-limiting thought patterns.

Clearing the clutter can be effective: A research review from Johns Hopkins found meditation to be on par with medication for relieving anxiety and depression symptoms. Small trials also suggest meditation can lower blood pressure, alleviate pain, reduce chronic inflammation and bolster immunity. A study by Massachusetts General Hospital found that as few as eight weeks of meditation not only helped people feel calmer, but also produced positive changes in areas of the brain responsible for memory, empathy and stress regulation.

Meditation is typically associated with stillness—sitting in a quiet space with your eyes closed and focusing on the breath—but rhythmic, repetitive movements can also focus the mind.

There are other, less-formal ways to meditate as well. "While we may experience mindfulness meditation during portions of a yoga class, we have opportunities to incorporate it in our daily lives," Wirtz says. "We can integrate it into many of our daily tasks, such as washing dishes, brushing our teeth or showering. In this method we would notice sensations we experience and how those make us feel."

Meditation can also be practiced while taking a walk, either by breathing mindfully or being openly aware of your surroundings. "Keep your eyes lifted as you walk, open up your peripheral vision and notice every step you take," Gagen advises, noting that you might apply a mantra as well—for example, saying "let" on the inhale and "go" on the exhale.

Just like any exercise, the most powerful benefits of meditation come from regular, daily practice. Set aside five minutes at first, and then gradually increase to 10 or 15 minutes at a specific time each day.

Not sure which practice will be most beneficial to you? Consider trying them all and seeing what sticks. "All three disciplines are sustainable, they can be modified as you evolve, and the journeys are endless," says Gagen. Best of all, they complement each other. Meditation, whether still or in motion, can calm the mind and nervous system. Core-focused Pilates can make yoga inversions, twists and balancing postures feel easier and more enjoyable, she says. "And then there's yoga, which works the whole body, and with regular practice begins to shine light on your life off your mat." No pain, all gain. ❧

ASK THE EXPERT

Q What's the difference between mat and equipment Pilates?

A The massive contraptions found in many Pilates studios may seem like medieval torture machines, but they're anything but. The exercises you're used to doing in mat class are essentially the same, but can feel entirely different on a Reformer. "In equipment classes, limbs are stabilized by a solid surface," says instructor Linda Wirtz. "This helps with alignment so you're working both sides more equally and with greater control." The apparatus also allows you to vary the difficulty and gives you greater feedback—if your form is incorrect, you'll feel it immediately and the equipment won't work the way you need it to. You'll probably be asked to take a few private sessions to learn the basics before you can take a group apparatus class.

Mat classes are almost always group classes, and are offered in gyms and YMCAs as well as at Pilates studios. And though they might be tougher at first—you don't have the equipment to give you an assist and you have to do all the "work" yourself—they're much less expensive and more accessible.

Bringing the tips of the thumb and index finger together is known as gyan mudra, and is the most common hand position in yoga (it's also often used in meditation).

HELPFUL HABITS FOR HAPPIER DAYS

Shaking up your A.M. routine can transform your whole life.

If you drag yourself out of bed every morning before starting the whirlwind of making your kids breakfast and getting them out the door, it's time for a reboot: How you begin your morning sets the tone for the rest of the day. "Without a morning ritual, you inadvertently put yourself in a passive and reactive role for the rest of your day," explains Jackie Gartman, a life coach in Woodland Hills, California. "But when you have good morning habits, you not only feel better, you're more likely to do your best work and be more productive—at work, home and in all the places that matter." Try all or some of these simple practices to help you get the day off to a calm but productive start:

SET YOUR ALARM A FEW MINUTES EARLIER

One of the easiest ways to make sure you start your day off with a positive mindset is to practice gratitude, advises Leah Remillet, a business-success strategist in Leavenworth, Washington. She personally sets her alarm for eight minutes before she needs to get up. "Once your alarm goes off, hit snooze and spend the next eight minutes thinking about and visualizing all you're grateful for, and how you want your day to unfold for you," she recommends.

If you're getting stuck, another option is to make a mental list of at least five things from the previous day that went well for you, whether it was lunch with a good friend or having a tickle fight with your toddler. "It might take some thinking, because when our minds are preoccupied with worry, it takes a little practice to see the shiny bits," explains David Stone, a life coach, transformational speaker and co-founder of I-Fearless Media Group in Cape Coral, Florida. But once you find them, it'll give you the self-confidence you need to go out and start your day.

PRACTICE SOME BREATHING

Taking five minutes to do some deep-breathing exercises will help you relax and allow you to supercharge your mornings with focus and ease, says Tessa Jenkins, a yoga instructor and manager of Bulldog Yoga Studio in Philadelphia. She recommends alternate-nostril breathing, a technique in which you take turns inhaling through one nostril and exhaling through the other. A study published in the journal *Biomedical Research International* found that people who practiced alternate-nostril breathing lowered their stress and anxiety levels compared to a control group. For more on how to do this, plus other deep-breathing methods, see page 40.

BE PRESENT IN THE SHOWER

We know your family may be waiting, but if you are able to, take some time to savor even a quick three-minute shower, advises Jaime Zuckerman,

Waking up before your kids get you up? Use the time to get yourself in a healthy place.

One mindfulness
exercise to try in the
shower: Envision the
water washing away
negative thoughts.

PhD, a Philadelphia psychologist. Close your eyes and feel the water cascade over your body, noticing its sound and temperature, the smell of the soap and how your scalp feels when you massage in the shampoo. "When you find your thoughts drifting off to something else, bring yourself gently back to the feel of the water," she advises.

SAGE YOURSELF

Rub white sage incense sticks (easy to find on Amazon) over your whole body, including the top of your head, around your arms, legs and under your feet. It may sound kooky, but it has both physical and spiritual benefits. "Sage has antimicrobial properties and has been shown to reduce airborne bacteria," explains Kim Julen, a feng shui expert in Kihei, Hawaii. "Energetically, it clears the air of stuck energy that can accumulate after, say, an argument."

SURROUND YOURSELF WITH SOME MORNING GREENERY

Research by NASA has found that houseplants can remove up to 87 percent of air toxins in 24 hours, and a study published in the *Journal of the American Society for Horticultural Science* found that even just sitting next to an indoor plant can help lower stress levels. New York City resident Lena Braun is a

WORKERS WHO HAD PLANTS IN THEIR OFFICES REPORTED 37 PERCENT LESS TENSION AND ANXIETY, 58 PERCENT LESS DEPRESSION AND 44 PERCENT LESS ANGER AND HOSTILITY."

UNIVERSITY OF TECHNOLOGY, SYDNEY

THINGS YOU SHOULD AVOID DOING IN THE MORNING

These habits can derail your best intentions.

→ HOPPING ON SOCIAL MEDIA
Right after waking up, you might feel the urge to check your email or Facebook. Don't. It can derail your morning—and your day—by giving you things to stress about or making you feel bad, says Sam Whittaker, a life coach in San Diego. You're far better off spending time with the human (or furry) members of your household instead.

→ SCRAMBLING TO PLAN YOUR DAY This can add to your morning stress, explains Don Dulin, a personal-development expert in Richmond, Texas. Instead, he recommends taking five to 10 minutes to do this the night before. "This way, when it's time to work, you don't spend 30 minutes trying to figure out what the important things are," he says.

→ HAVING AN INTENSE FAMILY CONVERSATION If you get into an argument—or even just a spirited debate—it will stay with you the rest of the day, causing you to ruminate about it instead of focusing on what you need to get done. (Who hasn't replayed those conversations over and over in their head?) Keep the subject light, focusing on laughter and love.

green believer: She eats breakfast surrounded by over 50 plants at her kitchen table. "The plants really help us deal with the daily pollution and stress associated with busy cities," she explains. "I guess you could call it plant-feng shui." Opt for rounded leaves, like monstera, philodendron or jade tree, which have a more calming effect, combined with some more colorful plants, she advises.

EAT A STRATEGIC BREAKFAST

"Eating a healthy breakfast not only gives you energy to start the day, it also significantly improves your concentration and attention," explains Zuckerman. Having high-protein fare like eggs or yogurt can help keep blood sugar levels steady, which in turn impacts energy, according to a study in the *American Journal of Clinical Nutrition*. If you need your morning java, by all means have it, but try to make it half decaf, half regular. "Caffeine can often lead to a 'crash' a few hours after consumption, which triggers a sudden drop in energy," Zuckerman explains.

TAKE A MOMENT TO MAKE A CONNECTION

It's so easy to get wrapped up in getting out the door that you forget to check in with your family or pets before you leave. But spending a few minutes playing with your dog or kids can help you (and them) feel centered and grounded all day long, explains Gartman. "I encourage people to share their intentions for the day with one another," she advises. Start off by asking your loved ones what they want to feel, and then follow up with asking them ways they think they can create those feeling states.

DRIVE THE SAME MORNING ROUTE

Take the same way to work, school drop-off or exercise class every day if possible. "When we can predict what comes next, our concentration, attention and memory are typically at their best," Zuckerman explains. "The familiar route every morning requires far less cognitive ability. This helps conserve your cognitive resources for later in the day." ❧

Eat up! A study from the University of California, Davis found women who skipped breakfast had elevated levels of stress hormones.

"A mom's hug lasts long after she lets go."
UNKNOWN

"Motherhood: All love begins and ends there."
ROBERT BROWNING

"Sometimes the strength of motherhood is greater than natural laws."
BARBARA KINGSOLVER

WORDS OF WISDOM

A sampling of some of our favorite quotes about motherhood.

"Mother's love is peace. It need not be acquired, it need not be deserved."
ERICH FROMM

"Having kids—the responsibility of rearing good, kind, ethical, responsible human beings—is the biggest job anyone can embark on."
MARIA SHRIVER

"A MOTHER UNDERSTANDS WHAT A CHILD DOES NOT SAY."
JEWISH PROVERB

"THERE'S NO WAY TO BE A PERFECT MOTHER AND A MILLION WAYS TO BE A GOOD ONE."

JILL CHURCHILL

"If evolution really works, how come mothers only have two hands?"

MILTON BERLE

"When you are a mother, you are never really alone in your thoughts. A mother always has to think twice—once for herself and once for her child."

SOPHIA LOREN

"Biology is the least of what makes someone a mother."

OPRAH WINFREY

"A mother's arms are made of tenderness, and children sleep soundly in them."

VICTOR HUGO

"God could not be everywhere, and therefore he made mothers."

RUDYARD KIPLING

"LIFE DOESN'T COME WITH A MANUAL; IT COMES WITH A MOTHER."

UNKNOWN

CHAPTER

EXPRESS YOURSELF

WRITING DOWN YOUR THOUGHTS CAN
PROFOUNDLY BENEFIT YOUR OVERALL WELL-BEING,
AND YOU DON'T HAVE TO SPEND A LOT OF TIME
TO SEE THE DIFFERENCE IT CAN MAKE.

THE WRITE STUFF

Reap major physical and mental benefits with just a few minutes of journaling a day.

t's associated with junior high kids (remember the diary with the lock and key?) and artists (Virginia Woolf, Anaïs Nin), but it turns out everyone should consider keeping a journal. It can significantly lower your levels of stress, depression and anxiety; speed healing; enhance your immune system; lessen the symptoms of some chronic illnesses and help you sleep better. And all you need to do is write (and you don't even have to have Maya Angelou's way with words).

Doctors and scientists call it expressive writing while "regular" people call it journaling: Either

A UCLA study found that putting feelings into words had therapeutic effects, making subjects' emotions of sadness, anger and pain seem less intense.

Many people like a journal that is small enough to slip in a bag, so they can jot down thoughts as they arise.

"BY WRITING, YOU PUT SOME STRUCTURE AND ORGANIZATION TO THOSE ANXIOUS FEELINGS. IT HELPS YOU TO GET PAST THEM."

JAMES PENNEBAKER, PHD

way, it's simply the regular practice of recording your thoughts, feelings, anxieties and desires. Its many benefits have been confirmed by numerous studies, most notably by James Pennebaker, PhD, the Regents Centennial Professor of Psychology at the University of Texas at Austin and author of numerous books on the subject, including *Opening Up by Writing It Down: How Expressive Writing Improves Health and Eases Emotional Pain*. His notable 1988 study of 50 undergrads found that those who wrote about traumatic experiences each day for four days were less likely to get sick and more likely to be in "positive moods." Pennebaker also interviewed over 60 Holocaust survivors, noting that those who were more open and revealing were healthier a year later than those who were so-called "low disclosers."

"There are hundreds of studies that find [expressive writing] benefits health and subjective well-being," acknowledges Beth Jacobs, PhD, a clinical psychologist with an expertise in therapeutic writing and the author of *Writing for Emotional Balance: A Guided Journal to Help You Manage Overwhelming Emotions*. Over the past 30-plus years, Jacobs, who teaches an online course through the International Association for Journal Writing, has observed "critical benefits you can prove to yourself right away."

The first one is clarity, she says. "By journaling, you're forced to articulate your internal process to a greater degree." Secondly, writing in a journal gives you perspective. "You're viewing your own self from a little distance and with a little detachment. It helps you realize that something is just a thought. It will come, it will go and there will be another one." The third benefit is emotional release. "You're doing a motor activity that is connected with your inner working, and it's a release."

SET YOUR OWN RULES

Jacobs has some simple tips for getting started. "Think of it as a self-indulgence, not an assignment," she advises. Second, don't think you need to stick to any specific guidelines. If you like writing with a pen, use a pen. If you like a keyboard, type your thoughts on your computer. "Also, start in small

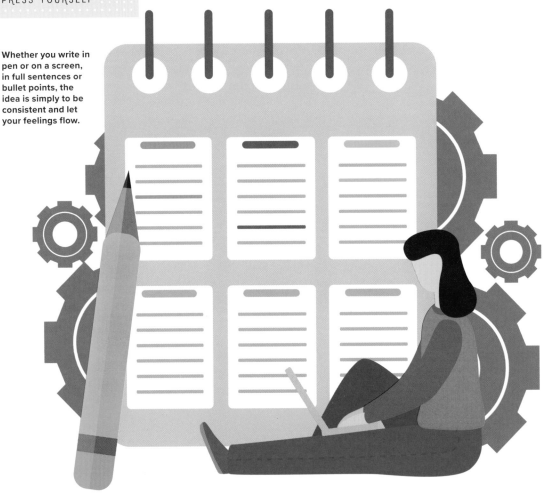

Whether you write in pen or on a screen, in full sentences or bullet points, the idea is simply to be consistent and let your feelings flow.

increments," she says. "Write one page or for 10 minutes, whatever is easier for you." Finally, "Don't pause too much, especially in the beginning. Think of it as an emotion that keeps going. You really want to be focused on the process, not the product."

TROUBLESHOOTING TIPS

Getting stuck or bored is inevitable, but not the end of the world. When this happens, Jacobs suggests shaking things up. "Pretend you're starting over. Get a new journal; try a new method." For example, those who usually write long, freehand pages might switch to bullet-point lists. "Or reread a past entry as though you had found it floating in the street on a piece of paper, not one you wrote

yourself. Identify three things in that entry that you wonder about, that could be different avenues to explore."

For those who find they're not making journaling a priority, Jacobs suggests writing an entry about what you love about your journal and what you hate about it. "Go right into the ambivalence. It's telling you something—don't fight it," she says.

And that fear of being discovered, of having someone read your most private, personal thoughts? It's very valid. "The best thing to do is not inform anybody that you're journaling, so nobody pokes around," she says. "Be discreet, tuck them away. I had one client who kept journals in the trunk of the car." ❧

HELP—I CAN'T WRITE!

Grammar and spelling don't matter when you're journaling.

Thanks to emails and texts, most of us actually spend the better part of our day writing—it's become ingrained in our culture as a primary form of communication. But self-doubt or full-on writer's block can strike even the most seasoned diarists, says journal designer Laura Rubin, who leads journaling workshops and is a devoted twice-a-day journaler. Here, her tips for overcoming your writing phobia.

→ **UNDERSTAND THE DIFFERENCE BETWEEN JOURNALING AND WRITING** "I sometimes hear, 'I'm bad at journaling' but there is no bad, there is just 'do,'" says Rubin. "You don't need to be a good writer to be good at journaling— you're not writing a novel, you're just putting words on paper, which, in and of itself, is incredibly therapeutic. If there's an interesting glimmer in there that you decide to explore further, that's great, but there doesn't need to be."

→ **LET YOURSELF GO** "Remind yourself that there is no audience for what you're writing," she says. "Grammar, spelling, even penmanship—none of that is important here. Fun fact: The word 'essay' comes from the French verb *essayer*, which means 'to try.' Give yourself permission to try without judging your output. There's no need to reread your writing; when you're finished, you can shut your notebook and walk away."

→ **TAKE ADVANTAGE OF PROMPTS** "Sometimes it's easier to start writing if you have a jumping-off point," Rubin says. "I keep some books of poetry that I like handy— Joy Harjo, Mary Oliver and Hafiz are some of my favorites. I flip open to a random page, read the poem and then use that as my inspiration." We've got plenty of prompts, beginning on page 88.

→ **MAKE A LIST** "I often hear from people who say they don't journal but they make lists, and I remind them that lists are actually a potent and helpful device for journaling," Rubin notes. "For example, try out a sense-check exercise where you write out what you're feeling via all five senses (what you're tasting, touching, smelling, hearing and seeing). It's a simple way to drop yourself into your body and be present. A gratitude list is another easy way to lift your mood; use all five senses as a filter of what you're most grateful for.

At a loss for words? Try meditating before writing in your journal.

Journaling allows us to work through issues and come to a place of peace and clarity about how to move forward, says Shilagh Mirgain, PhD. But it doesn't have to be an arduous process.

OVERCOMING JOURNALING ROADBLOCKS

Even the most prolific writers can get stuck. When you need a little extra motivation, try these tips.

Does the thought of starting a journal page make you freeze up in terror? You're not alone—many famous writers have suffered from writer's block, from F. Scott Fitzgerald to Charles M. Schulz, best known as the creator of *Peanuts*. If you've ever decided to take up a journal practice and find yourself sitting in front of a blank page and then...sitting...you know the feeling. Faced with creating the follow-up novel to *The Great Gatsby* or drawing your umpteenth comic strip, this kind of paralysis may be easy to understand, and perhaps it's even expected. But a personal journal? Shouldn't it be a little easier?

The problem may actually be that we have some misconceptions about journaling: For one thing, you may have lost sight of the real mental and physical benefits that it can offer, says Kathy Hardie-Williams, MEd, MS, a family therapist based in Tigard, Oregon.

"Research shows that journaling is an effective tool for releasing negative emotions, finding gratitude and reducing stress," she explains. "I believe it's good for my mental health because it helps me put things in perspective. I struggle with the same challenges that others do; I'll make a commitment and then sometimes fail to keep up with it. But I've become much better at giving myself compassion and allowing myself to pick up where I left off."

Keeping a journal may also strengthen your sense of self and boost your confidence. "As a culture, we tend to look externally for answers," says Shilagh Mirgain, PhD, distinguished psychologist at the School of Medicine and Public Health at University of Wisconsin-Madison. "Journaling helps us tap into our innate wisdom; it's a great way to stay resilient during challenging times." If you've hit a roadblock in your journal practice, here's how to get back on track:

MAKE A DATE

Creating an actual appointment in your calendar, complete with reminder alerts, can help you stay accountable to your journaling practice and establish it as a bona fide to-do. You might make it part of your bedtime or morning routine so that it becomes as natural a part of your daily life as brushing your teeth. "It's also really nice to schedule with your family," suggests Mirgain. "It's a great thing for parents and kids to do, side by side. Just say, 'Hey, let's get out a piece of paper and a pen and do 10 minutes of journaling as a family exercise.' And then people can share what they feel comfortable with."

SET A TIMER

Sometimes it can feel like there's not enough time in the day to accomplish every type of self-care we're advised to take up. There's the daily exercise, the healthy-meal prep, the meditation, the skin care, the Netflix and chill…. It can seriously seem overwhelming, especially when you've got a whole family to take care of, let alone yourself. One solution is to give yourself permission for brevity. "When we look at the therapeutic benefits of journaling, research shows that even just doing a few minutes of expressive writing can help," Mirgain says. "You don't have to sit down for 30 minutes and write a whole chapter. Instead, just doing two to three minutes at a designated time can be useful."

STICK TO ONE SENTENCE A DAY

If even three minutes sounds like too much to spare, consider restricting your expressive writing to just a single sentence. "It's about meeting yourself where you are," says Hardie-Williams. "Writing one sentence helps to keep the habit of journaling going—and eventually, you may find yourself writing more than that." You might also consider using an actual calendar as your journal; watching each day fill up can be incredibly motivating.

START WITH A QUESTION

"If all you can think of to write about are the details of what you had for breakfast, that's fine," says Hardie-Williams. But a journal filled with oatmeal and coffee probably isn't exactly what you had in mind when you decided to start writing. To give some structure and prompt your initial entries, consider asking yourself a question. It can be as simple as, How did I feel today? or, What is the first word that comes to mind today? or, What am I grateful for? You can use your journal time to answer the question until you get used to the rhythm and routine of a daily practice. "It's like anything else: The more you do it, the more confident you become and eventually, you will feel a sense of mastery," says Hardie-Williams. With ideas like writing about your favorite teacher, or describing the room you're sitting in, you can add variety to your practice. For more inspiration, check out the prompts beginning on page 88.

JOURNALING HELPS US TAP INTO OUR INNER VOICE THAT ALWAYS HAS OUR BEST INTERESTS AT HEART."

SHILAGH MIRGAIN, PHD

Don't let time constraints be a deterrent. Writing just a few minutes a day will be beneficial.

Expressive writing
can help you see
things in a new light.

SILENCE YOUR INNER CRITIC

Nothing can kill the mood like your inner English teacher critiquing your grammar and spelling. "It's important to mute that voice, or acknowledge it for what it is and give yourself permission to write freely, allowing the words to flow so you're getting out whatever is coming up," says Mirgain. "When we write, we're expressing the full range of emotions, which is one of the most direct paths for self-knowledge and helps you make sense of your current situation, work through issues and get clarity on concerns." What's more, there's no need to stick to a particular method of writing. You don't even have to write full sentences; consider switching it up by writing bullet points and numbered entries, or incorporating drawings.

STOP WHEN IT HURTS

When we're going through an especially difficult experience, like a divorce or recovering from trauma, writing can actually reintroduce stress and amplify your sense of being overwhelmed. If that happens, by all means, stop and shift direction. Hardie-Williams suggests channeling these negative feelings into more constructive avenues for personal growth. "Ask yourself how you can use this difficult experience to become a better person. You can also explore solutions that are within your control, such as increasing your exposure to more positive experiences. Try to avoid writing about the anger and feelings of being overwhelmed to the point of brooding about them. It's healthy to write about things that are bothering you, but you also want to move on to the positive things."

REWARD YOURSELF

Have you successfully written for seven days straight? That's worth a new lipstick, a luxurious bubble bath or (insert your favorite treat here). Setting up a reward system for writing in your journal on a regular basis can help you connect the act of writing with something you already perceive as pleasurable, so you'll be more likely to want to settle down with pen and paper. 🌺

PRIVATE PRACTICE

The fear of having one's innermost thoughts be revealed can be a major impediment to a journaling practice.

Some people are concerned that their journal entries might be read by someone else. "I know one person who made a pact with a friend that if she ever passed away, the friend would burn her journal," says Shilagh Mirgain, PhD, who suggests buying a notebook with a lock on it if you're worried about someone reading it.

Another way to maintain your privacy is to destroy your entries afterward. "There can be benefit to reviewing what you write months or even years later, but often the value is in the writing itself rather than the reflection. I personally have people write and then shred it. I even had a patient toss the pages into a bonfire—which was quite cathartic."

loving
MOTHERHOOD

What are five of your favorite things about being a mom?

1
2
3
4
5

What are some things you may have been surprised
to find enjoyable?

What made you most happy about being a mom today?

taking a
DO-OVER

What was one parenting frustration that you faced today?

_____
_____
_____
_____
_____

Take a few moments to look at this from a new perspective.
What are some things you might have done to handle
the situation differently?

_____
_____
_____
_____

What else might you be able to do the next time to avoid
this same frustration?

_____
_____
_____
_____
_____

making MEMORIES

What are some things you would most want your kids to remember about their childhood?

_____
_____
_____
_____
_____
_____
_____

What do you most want them to remember about you as a mom?

_____
_____
_____
_____
_____
_____
_____
_____

facing CHALLENGES

What things have you found to be particularly hard
when it comes to parenting?

_____

_____

_____

_____

_____

What can you try doing to make them a little easier?

_____

_____

_____

_____

Where can you find some support in helping
to deal with these challenges?

_____

_____

_____

_____

_____

me, myself
AND I

What are a few things you wish your kids knew about you?

_____

_____

_____

_____

_____

What words would they use to describe you to their friends?

_____

_____

_____

What would you want to share with your kids about
your own childhood?

_____

_____

_____

_____

play TIME!

What are five fun things that you want to try with your family in the next couple of months?

1 _____

2 _____

3 _____

4 _____

5 _____

What appeals to you most about these activities?

_____

_____

_____

What actions can you take to make them happen?

_____

_____

_____

_____

celebrating the SMALL MOMENTS

What things made you laugh today with your children?

_____

_____

_____

_____

_____

What else made you smile?

_____

_____

_____

_____

What one moment would you like to capture from today?

_____

_____

_____

_____

_____

life LESSONS

What are some new things that your child/children
have taught you in the past week?

_____
_____
_____
_____
_____
_____

What are some ways that you have grown since becoming a mom?

_____
_____
_____
_____

What life lessons has motherhood given you?

_____
_____
_____
_____

future SELVES

What are three things that you hope for
your child's/children's future?

1 _____

2 _____

3 _____

Picture your child/children as adults.
What characteristics do you hope they have?

_____

_____

_____

_____

What are some ways you can best help them develop
these characteristics?

_____

_____

_____

_____

being your
BEST

Write down a few times when you felt like you were
your best parenting self.

_____

_____

_____

_____

What do these situations have in common?

_____

_____

_____

How would you best describe yourself as a parent?

_____

_____

_____

_____

a fulfilled LIFE

What makes for a satisfying life?

_____

_____

_____

_____

_____

_____

In what ways is your life rewarding?

_____

_____

_____

_____

What is missing—and what are some steps you can take
to get those things into your life?

_____

_____

_____

_____

realizing your
POTENTIAL

Make a list of a few of your strengths.

1

2

3

4

5

How can these empower you to change things in your life?

GOALS

What's one objective you'd like to achieve
in the next six months?

_____

_____

_____

_____

In the next year?

_____

_____

_____

_____

In the next decade?

_____

_____

_____

_____

_____

positive
THINKING

What three things do you wish had never happened to you?

1

2

3

What lessons can you take away from those situations?

the power of KINDNESS

What impact can kindness have on the world?

_____

_____

_____

_____

_____

Make a kindness resolution. How can you be kinder
in the future?

_____

_____

_____

_____

How can that change your life?

_____

_____

_____

_____

_____

SELF-COMPASSION

Are there past experiences that you feel guilty about?
What are they?

_____

_____

_____

_____

_____

How do they affect or limit your life today?

_____

_____

_____

_____

Were there any extenuating circumstances that
would allow you to forgive yourself?

_____

_____

_____

_____

tackling YOUR FEARS

What are the five things you're most afraid of?

1 _____

2 _____

3 _____

4 _____

5 _____

Now list five major challenges that you've overcome.

1 _____

_____

2 _____

_____

3 _____

_____

4 _____

_____

5 _____

_____

Does knowing you've been able to get through these hard times give you confidence about facing future challenges?

_____

_____

_____

GOOD mornings

How do you want to feel when you wake up every day?

_____

_____

_____

_____

Journal about how your perfect day would be.
What would you do, with whom would you spend time?

_____

_____

_____

_____

_____

_____

Is there at least one of these things you can do today?

_____

_____

_____

_____

HAPPINESS

What are some nonmaterial ways you have achieved
success in your life?

_____

_____

_____

_____

_____

_____

_____

_____

Which one are you most proud of? What does it represent?

_____

_____

_____

_____

_____

_____

letting go of
JUDGMENT

How often do you criticize others? What compels
you to speak negatively about them?

_____

_____

_____

_____

_____

How does this make you feel?

_____

_____

_____

_____

Would you feel better if you were more compassionate?

_____

_____

_____

_____

good KARMA

What was the last kind thing you did for someone without hoping for something in return?

_____

_____

_____

_____

_____

How did it make you feel?

_____

_____

_____

_____

Is there a time when you wish you could have been kinder?

_____

_____

_____

_____

_____

How can your actions change the world?

_____

_____

_____

_____

_____

LOOKING BACK

Make a list of five memories that always make you happy. Why do they make you smile?

1

2

3

4

5

three WISHES

What three wishes do you have for your life?

1 _____

_____

2 _____

_____

3 _____

_____

How would your life be different if they came true?

1 _____

_____

2 _____

_____

3 _____

_____

What three wishes do you have for the world?

1 _____

_____

2 _____

_____

3 _____

_____

a line a day REFLECTIONS

Write a sentence about how you're feeling every day for a week.

_____

Sunday

_____

_____

_____

Monday

_____

_____

Tuesday

Wednesday

Thursday

Friday

Saturday

the ABCs of GRATITUDE

Many people say that the first step to happiness is to appreciate what you have. For each letter of the alphabet, write down something you're grateful for.

A _____

B _____

C _____

D _____

E _____

F _____

G _____

H

I

J

K

L

M

N

O

P

Q

R

S

T

U

V

W

X

Y

Z

finding
PEACE

Do a word-association exercise with the word serenity.

_____

_____

_____

Write down all the words that pop into your head
when you think of tranquility.

_____

_____

_____

_____

_____

What did this exercise reveal to you?

_____

_____

_____

_____

_____

_____

CREDITS

COVER marabird/Getty Images. SpicyTruffel/Getty Images **2–3** fizkes/Getty Images **4–5** YakobchukOlena/Getty Images **6–7** Ezra Bailey/Getty Images **8–9** Westend61/Getty Images **10–11** gradyreese/Getty Images **12–13** Halfpoint/Getty Images **14–15** Visit Roemvanitch/Getty Images **16–17** WANDER WOMEN COLLECTIVE/Getty Images **18–19** KatarzynaBialasiewicz/Getty Images **20–21** *From left:* Emely/Getty Images. exopixel/shutterstock.mayakova/shutterstock **22–23** Emely/Getty Images **24–25** Kerkez/Getty Images **26–27** golubovy/Getty Images **28–29** *From left:* Jessica Peterson/Getty Images. Jamie Grill/Getty Images **30–31** adamkaz/Getty Images **32–33** LaylaBird/Getty Images **34–35** fizkes/Getty Images **36–37** Ridofranz/Getty Images **38–39** *From left:* YakobchukOlena/Getty Images. Luis Alvarez/Getty Images **40–41** Choochart Choochaikupt/EyeEm/Getty Images **42–43** Anchalee Phanmaha/Getty Images **44–45** Shestock/Getty Images **46–47** LENblR/Getty Images **48–49** Zero Creatives/Getty Images **50–51** stockfour/shutterstock **52–53** Rawpixel/Getty Images **54–55** *From left:* Melissa Ross/Getty Images. Emma Kim/Getty Images **56–57** JGI/Jamie Grill/Getty Images **58–59** Illustrations: Babkina Svetlana/Shutterstock. Eva-Katalin/Getty Images **60–61** *From left:* Jamie Grill/Getty Images. Thomas Northcut/Getty Images **62–63** Peathegee Inc/Getty Images **64–65** wundervisuals/Getty Images **66–67** Tara Moore/Getty Images **68–69** Youngoldman/Getty Images **70–71** gradyreese/Getty Images **72–73** *Clockwise from top left:* Agence Opale/Alamy Stock Photo. Historic Images / Alamy Stock Photo. AF archive/Alamy Stock Photo (2). AF Fotografie/Alamy Stock Photo. GL Archive/Alamy Stock Photo. Vera Anderson/Getty images. Jeff Vespa/Getty Images. Denver Post /Getty Images **74–75** Dean Drobot/shutterstock **76–77** hisa_nishiya/shutterstock **78–79** hisa_nishiya/shutterstock **80–81** *From left:* yellowdesign/getty images. hisa_nishiya/shutterstock **82–83** cosmaa/shutterstock **84–85** cosmaa/shutterstock **86–87** cosmaa/shutterstock **88–89** *From left:* Elena Melnikova/Shutterstock.Tatyana Antusenok/Gettty Images **90–91** NKTN/Getty Images **92–93** *From left:* Irtsya/shutterstock.bluebearry/Getty Images **94–95** *From left:* Marina Malades/shutterstock.Dmitrii Musku/Getty Images **96–97** *From left:* mirrelley/shutterstock.ma_rish/Getty Images **98–99** TeraVector/shutterstock **100–101** *From left:* Nicetoseeya/shutterstock.NotionPic/shutterstock **102–103** *From left:* Anastezia Luneva/shutterstock.Alina Kvaratskhelia/Getty Images **104–105** *From left:* Svetlana Iris/shutterstock.Dar_ria/Getty Images **106–107** *From left:* Maria_Galybina/shutterstock. Barrirret/Getty Images **108–109** GoodStudio/shutterstock **110–111** *From left:* Anna Paff/shutterstock. Varlamova Lydmila/shutterstock **112–113** *From left:* Olya Fedorova/shutterstock.naum/shutterstock **114–115** tonia_tkach/shutterstock **116–117** *From left:* Alina Sagirova/shutterstock. Nnena Irina/shutterstock **118–119** *From left:* LuFei/shutterstock.Zaie/shutterstock **120–121** *From left:* Natallia Novik/shutterstock.Mary Long/shutterstock **122–123** *From left:* Jamie Soon Design/shutterstock. artem_mortem/shutterstock **124–125** Lera Efremova/shutterstock **126–127** *From left:* subbery/shutterstock. lilac/shutterstock **128–129** *From left:* TairA/shutterstock. ZUBKOVA IULIIA/shutterstock **130–131** *From left:* ugina/shutterstock. Nicetoseeya/shutterstock **132–133** *From left:* vavavka/shutterstock. Alexandra Romanova/shutterstock **134–135** *From left:* Tanor/shutterstock. GoodStudio/shutterstock **136–137** *From left:* GoodStudio/shutterstock. anemad/shutterstock **138–139** Juliana Brykova/shutterstock **SPINE** marabird/Getty Images **BACK COVER** SpicyTruffel/Getty Images

---

SPECIAL THANKS TO CONTRIBUTING WRITERS

Barbara Brody
Kimberly Goad
AJ Hanley
Nancy Hawley
Hallie Levine
Leah McLaughlin
Kate Rope
Rima Sugi

CENTENNIAL BOOKS

An Imprint of
Centennial Media, LLC
40 Worth St., 10th Floor

New York, NY 10013, U.S.A.
CENTENNIAL BOOKS is a trademark of Centennial Media, LLC

ISBN 978-1-951274-58-0

Distributed by
Simon & Schuster, Inc.
1230 Avenue of the Americas
New York, NY 10020, U.S.A.

For information about custom editions, special sales and premium and corporate purchases,
please contact Centennial Media at contact@centennialmedia.com.

Manufactured in China

10 9 8 7 6 5 4 3 2 1

Publishers & Co-Founders Ben Harris, Sebastian Raatz
Editorial Director Annabel Vered
Creative Director Jessica Power
Executive Editor Janet Giovanelli
Deputy Editors Ron Kelly, Alyssa Shaffer
Design Director Martin Elfers
Senior Art Director Pino Impastato
Art Directors Runyon Hall, Natali Suasnavas, Joseph Ulatowski
Copy/Production Patty Carroll, Angela Taormina
Assistant Art Director Jaclyn Loney
Photo Editor April O'Neil
Production Manager Paul Rodina
Production Assistant Alyssa Swiderski
Editorial Assistant Tiana Schippa
Sales & Marketing Jeremy Nurnberg